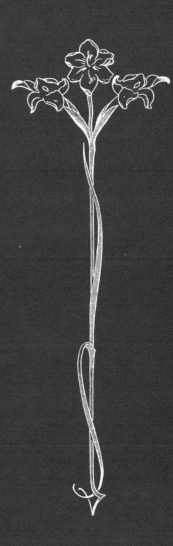

COUNTRY LIVING
MAGAZINE

Floral
INTERIORS

COUNTRY LIVING
M A G A Z I N E

Floral INTERIORS

decorative inspiration from nature

Judy Spours

C&B
COLLINS & BROWN

For my parents

First published in Great Britain in 2002
by Collins & Brown Limited
64 Brewery Road
London N7 9NT

A member of the Chrysalis Group plc

1 3 5 7 9 8 6 4 2

British Library Cataloguing-in-Publication Data:
A catalogue record for this book is available from the British Library.

ISBN 1 85585 940 8

Conceived, edited and designed by Collins & Brown Limited

Editor: Gillian Haslam
Copy Editor: Alison Wormleighton
Designer: Christine Wood

Reproduction by Classic Scan Pte Ltd, Singapore
Printed and bound in Hong Kong
This book was typeset using Neue Helvetica and Snell Roundhand

contents

foreword by Susy Smith
Editor of *Country Living* Magazine

Nature has been the primary inspiration for design and decoration for every civilisation. Think of Egypt's stylised papyrus, the acanthus leaves of ancient Greece and the tulips intricately woven into Turkish carpets.

A glance through the archives of some of Britain's best-known makers of fabrics and wall coverings – Colefax and Fowler, Sanderson, GP and J Baker – reveals the consistency with which floral symbolism has been used for home furnishings over the decades. Imagery ranges from wonderful fat, blowsy cabbage roses to delicate sprigs of daisy or forget-me-not. Designs are translated to suit a myriad of uses from heavyweight upholstery fabrics to cotton bedlinen and translucent sheers, from the finest china to the most robust floor tiles.

It comes as little surprise then to learn that of the hundreds of homes that have appeared in *Country Living* Magazine over the years, most have at least one room that has been inspired by flowers. This book is made up of a collection of the most beautiful of these interiors. Perhaps the most uplifting of all are those where the atmosphere of a room is set by a vase or bowl of the real thing – wild flowers from the hedgerow or a simple posy from the owner's garden. This, after all, is what *Country Living* Magazine is all about. We hope it inspires you.

Susy Smith

introduction

Decorating books and television programmes constantly promote the linking of indoor and outdoor living areas as though this is a new idea. However, houses have been designed with the intention of merging interior and exterior spaces since classical times. And where this has not been literally possible — often because of an inhospitable climate — elements of the wild and of gardens have always been introduced inside the house symbolically, as part of a decorative scheme.

Our homes now reflect a long history of naturalism in interior design. New, ecologically sound materials and strange organic forms jostle for position alongside textiles and ornament inspired by the gardens and landscapes of past cultures. This book takes a glimpse at some of these interior styles and objects. They may be traditional floral chintz fabrics, carpets depicting the walled gardens of the East, silverware hammered into the shape of fruits and vegetables or contemporary schemes that incorporate found objects from the wild. Even homes that are free of any floral motif may be decorated in colours inspired by garden flowers and foliage or the earth or sky outside our windows.

If we look back, we find that naturalistic pattern in ornamentation is common to every culture, ancient and modern and in all parts of the globe. From what remains of their decorations, we can see, for example, that the Egyptians used designs of lily and lotus and the ancient Greeks acanthus, honeysuckle, lily and holly. The Romans painted beautiful floral landscapes blooming with oleander, myrtle and rose on the walls of their villas and the stonemasons of early England carved roses and the foliage of indigenous oak, ivy, vine and blackberry on their buildings.

The further these developing cultures then moved away from a close connection with the wilderness surrounding them into secure urban settings, the more important

LEFT Early 19th-century transfer-printed teacups and saucers manufactured by the grand old English pottery firms of Wedgwood and Spode are decorated with flowering plants and with idealized landscapes. Although the patterns are heavily influenced by the contemporaneous vogue for Chinese ceramics, they have now come to appear quintessentially English.

LEFT Motifs from the garden constitute all of the pattern in this cool interior. A faded cotton chintz reminiscent of early 19th-century styles is used for a loose chair cover, and its cushion is covered in a later, more voluptuous Victorian chintz design.

RIGHT The gentle pastel colours of a hellebore — and of its grey-green foliage — indicate why English floral chintz is particularly prized when its colours have faded to similarly soft tones.

elements of the natural world as decoration became to them. Geographical distance from the real threats of the wild produced an enchantment with its more attractive side. In decoration, nature could be tamed and idealized — every leaf and flower could become perfect when drawn to decorate a wall or ornament a dinner plate. This tendency explains why the period of swift and intense industrialization in the 19th century was also the time when interiors were characterized by a greater profusion of floral styles than at any time previously. The decorative arts on view at the Great Exhibition in London in 1851, for example, were totally dominated by naturalistic decoration; flowers covered everything from wallpaper to ceramics, designed for city rooms that no longer looked out over the countryside.

From this history an interesting tale emerges. Motifs such as the daisy or the rose are found in decoration the world over, but they are differently drawn. The full-blown roses of English decoration contrast, for example, with the stylized petals of Indian designs. Then as the trade routes of the world opened up, the designs of one culture were adopted and modified by another, resulting in a fascinating mix of floral styles. These in turn developed against the backdrop of the spectacular growth in the West of domestic flower cultivation between the 16th and 19th centuries, as plant hunters returned with exotic flowers from all parts of the globe, providing a new floral vocabulary for artists and designers.

This book tracks this decorative progression, illustrating both the beautiful and the eccentric decorative arts that resulted. After chapters about the use of colours inspired by nature, about ceramics, textiles, surface decoration and ornament, the book ends with a look at the real elements of nature that we bring inside — flowers, foliage, berries, wood, pebbles, shells. It suggests that, in one way or another, our interiors are never that far away in style or content from the exterior landscape beyond their walls.

Natural
Colour

ABOVE Many contemporary paints are still coloured in a naturalistic earth palette of umber, ochre and pale celadon green.

PREVIOUS PAGES Earth colours shine through unadulterated in earthenware jugs, harmonizing with the rich browns of chopped wood and the gentle mauves of garden daisies.

Wherever we live in the world, our primary inspiration for the colours we use to decorate interior spaces comes from nature. The contrasts and harmonies of the colours we see outdoors are those that we have come to feel are right – that seem natural and uncontrived. Because the colours of nature differ according to geography, decorators in one culture will favour a spectrum quite different from that used by others. For example, the deciduous woods of a temperate climate display rich colours that change dramatically with the seasons, from the pale greens of spring through summer's dark greens to the vibrant yellows and reds of autumn. In a tropical area, however, the colours are of quite another intensity: rainforest flowers and fungi adopt the brilliant and iridescent colours that can be seen in the deep shade of the forest floor, hidden under a dense canopy of trees. Correspondingly, interiors in these contrasting areas of the world are traditionally decorated in colours that reflect the indigenous flora and that are created by natural dyes extracted from them.

It is almost impossible to imagine a natural world without colour to give character to the shape of things. Writing in 1873 about the principles of decoration, the influential designer Christopher Dresser, a keen student of nature as a designer and colourist, comments on the important relationship between colour and form. He concludes that colour is more important than shape in human perception. Formless colour can have great charm, but colourless form is dull and lifeless. He gives an example from nature:

'A sunset is entrancing when the sky glows with radiant hues; the blue is almost lost in red, the yellow is as a sea of transparent gold, and the whole presents a variety and blending of tints which charm, and soothe, and lull to reverie; and yet all form is indistinct and obscure.'

Nature is inconceivable in black and white – merely a toned collection of grey shapes – but its colours seen alone can be exciting and compelling. Similarly, interior decoration would be infinitely dull without natural colour to throw architecture and objects into relief. As Christopher Dresser says, 'Colour is the means by which we render form apparent.'

Not only has nature always been the starting point for colour ideas, but it has also been the source of actual colour to use as dye and paint throughout history. Pigment is drawn from the earth in the form of oxides and minerals, and is extracted from plants through the boiling of leaves, flowers and roots. These were the only ways of reproducing colour until the invention of synthetic, chemical dyes in the 19th century. No wonder, then, that interior colours have always closely reflected the hues of the exterior landscape – they are a real part of it.

BELOW LEFT A 'moodboard' explores potential decorating combinations of pastel English garden colours – the pale blues and yellows of midsummer flowers, backed by soft foliage greens.

BELOW This dainty interior scheme, in which real flowers are juxtaposed with floral textile prints and embroidery, is given a backdrop of palest green on the walls. The style is inspired by a garden, where the mix of bright flowers is tempered by the soft greens of surrounding foliage.

foliage

The starting point for decorating with natural colour has to be green, the dominant hue of nature, that of the foliage that enables plants to live. The most important natural pigment is chlorophyll, which makes plants green and allows them to photosynthesize. The other colours of plants are almost always seen against an overwhelming background of greens of every shade and intensity. These foliage colours are so familiar that their subtle gradations are instantly called to mind by the names we give them: leaf, grass, fern, moss, lettuce, palm, sage, mint, willow, fir, forest. Then there are the greens of fruits, nuts and vegetables that we also recognize in all their subtlety: olive, pea, avocado, lime, greengage, gooseberry, almond, apple, pistachio. They all comprise one basic colour, but we have a substantial vocabulary of its different qualities.

Green is characterized as the most balanced colour, taking its place between the warmth of red and the coolness of blue. The paler shades of green can be used for interior wall colour in imitation of the background of the natural world, particularly if colours and forms inspired by flowers and fruits are then introduced. Pale green gives a room an atmosphere of calm and equilibrium and the freshness of spring. Softer, grey-green shades are more reminiscent of summer foliage, and look

BELOW The colours and the forms of foliage, in a complex array of greens sliding into yellows and browns, are put together as samples in order to plan a decorating scheme. The textures of the fabrics also imitate nature, from the fine translucence of spring-green leaves to the coarseness of tree bark.

RIGHT A leaf-green painted bedroom gives the illusion of sleeping out in the woods. The green fabric canopy above the bed, like treetops overhead, enhances the effect in a room designed for a poetical green thought in a green shade.

BELOW Foliage and vegetables provide inspiration in the textured green and white shades of a pumpkin patch.

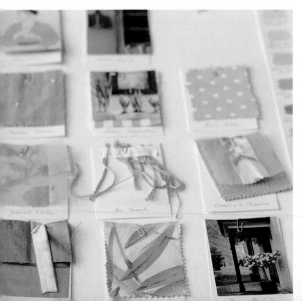

wonderful in rooms that open to the garden outside, blurring the boundaries between inside and out with colour.

Though dramatic-looking on walls, darker greens are more difficult to use as they can appear sombre, particularly if they have a matt rather than a glossy finish or if the light in the room is dim. Among the most problematic shades of green are dull olive and sage, but either shade can be brightened up by combining it with soft red or light yellow. Also difficult are vivid peacock greens, which have an exoticism that works better in strong tropical sun than in grey-tinged, northern light. It is best to resist, too, any temptation to paint a ceiling green, as the light it reflects down will make the occupants of a room look sickly.

The bright green shade of fresh, uncooked peas was very popular in the early 18th and the 19th centuries, while lime was fashionable with 20th-century modernists and is popular again today. If used with restraint, as accents or over small areas, these tangy fruit and vegetable colours can look marvellous, but lime in particular has a sharpness that makes it difficult to live with in large amounts.

green and blue
If foliage is the backdrop to the brighter colours of flowers and fruit, then the blue of the sky is the backdrop to the foliage, and the two together have a calmness and airiness that can light up an interior scheme. The greens used with blue should themselves contain more blue than yellow, so that they merge and harmonize. This is a surprisingly difficult combination to get right, and it is certainly essential that the blue and green chosen are of the same intensity – a bright royal blue would not work with a pale moss green, for example.

Blue and green meet in the shades that we call petrol blue, duck egg blue, teal and turquoise. They are the colours of water, of the sea, changing in the light to be sometimes blue, sometimes green, or even grey. Perhaps because of their mutability, they go in and out of fashion at high speed. Turquoise is the colour of the moment, with bright Caribbean aqua decorating walls and shining through the

ABOVE Leaf greens and sky blue, combined in simple gingham fabric and ceramics, are fresh and spring-like, while the cool mauve of the flowers links the green and blue beautifully.

LEFT Sky blue and light blue-green separated by white give the upper storey of a house a light, airy feeling, as though a summer sky is glimpsed through fresh young foliage. White paint on both floor and ceiling creates an impression that the rooms are floating somewhere high up.

translucent plastic of contemporary electrical goods, bath accessories and other everyday household items.

Some years ago, the prevalence of turquoise would have been unacceptable. For example, the contemporary design critic Basil Ionides, writing in 1926, is damning about blue-greens: 'Pale blue of a hedge-sparrow-egg tone was once used: it is never considered now by those of taste. It seems to have died out slowly, its last gasps being in cheap silk blouses.' Can this be the colour that was used by some of the great Renaissance architects and that is so popular again now?

green and red

In autumn, the leaves that have worked so hard to feed deciduous trees start to lose their green chlorophyll. First they turn yellow, as the green is replaced by the colour of the carotenoids that show through as chlorophyll breaks down. Then the carotenoids disintegrate to be replaced by the oranges and reds of anthocyanins and lipochromes. The combinations of greens, yellows, oranges and reds that result are staggeringly beautiful at this time of year, although, curiously, the bright leaf colours are of no use whatsoever to the tree.

Red and green used together in interior decoration are as powerfully contrasting a combination as they are in the autumn landscape. The two colours are direct spectral opposites, and when juxtaposed they can be quite challenging to the eye. A green object placed against a red background can appear indistinct, a visual trick which is explained by the opposing forces of the colours. If you stare intently at red in bright light, for example, then close your eyes, the colour that will appear to be on the inside of your eyelids is green.

Dark red with green is a formal decorating combination, historically used for picture galleries or rather grand dining rooms. Its strong contrast needs some help, with the introduction of border colours, such as black and gold, to divide up the combination, or of other, paler or patterned surfaces. Green and red interiors, though, can have all the drama of their wild inspiration.

ABOVE The vivid and dramatic colour contrasts of autumnal foliage offer decorating inspiration in the form of evergreens with berries, copper beech and the orange, scarlet and purple of changing deciduous leaves.

RIGHT A red room seen through the doorway of a green room sets up a strong contrast that defines the interior architecture. Quantities of white paint for ceilings and woodwork stop the colours becoming dazzling.

flowers

Flowers are the reproductive organs of plants, and as such they need to flaunt themselves in order to achieve their goal of fertilization. Sweet scent and, above all, eye-catching colour are invaluable in attracting the attentions of passing pollinating insects. With their infinite variety of form and colour – from the simplest yellow through reds and blues to elaborate confections of more than one hue – flowers have become objects of beauty, attracting the human eye and imagination as a side effect to their main purpose. Above all else in nature, flowers are our reference for a huge range of brilliant and surprising colours. They are imprinted on our minds – so indelibly that if we want to conjure up the idea of a certain shade, it is usually a flower that comes into mental view and its name that we cite as a description.

red and pink
Rose, cyclamen, fuchsia, blossom, poppy, carnation, geranium, raspberry, cerise, cranberry, cherry, tomato – once again, our colour vocabulary is delineated by the natural world. The fiery reds and calming pinks of

LEFT A brave and successful combination of red and pinks is dominated by bright fuchsia, undercut by dark red in the floral bedspread and lightened by the pale floral chintz curtains. A lively addition of other bright pinks and of mauve into the decorative equation prevents any risk of colour monotony.

BELOW Roses provide a natural blueprint for what might otherwise seem an almost impossibly exotic shade of bright pink.

BELOW A dusty, summery pink-and-red decorating scheme is planned out, and is brought into balance with suggestions for the inclusion of blue, yellow and green of the same tonal intensity.

garden flowers and fruits are used in interior design to add hot excitement or warm comfort in imitation of the world we see around us.

In efforts to reproduce the vibrancy of the colour, natural red pigments have long been derived from a number of sources. Certain lead oxides in the earth give shades of red, while the mineral cinnabar – more commonly referred to as vermilion, the pigment it produces – was used by artists in ancient China, Greece and Rome. Other historical sources of red include the kermes and cochineal insects, brazilwood and logwood, safflower and the root of the madder plant. Madder root was a primary source of alizarin, a pigment that could produce a fine bright scarlet, and for centuries madder was widely grown and cropped in Europe for this purpose. Later, in 1859, a vivid synthetic magenta was concocted. Though condemned by some as unnatural and tasteless, it did, in fact, provide a fair imitation of some of the brighter flowers, such as cyclamens and Mexican dahlias.

Correspondingly, red interior schemes can be either earthy and warm, or jangling with edgy bright colour. Combining a brownish red with a soft plaster pink gives a comforting environment, while a mix of scarlet and magenta is vivid and lively, though hardly restful. White can be used to offset red, particularly a strong primary shade that would otherwise be too fiery and assertive. Or red can be combined with a sunny strong yellow to give an opulent feel to a room.

The range of pinks used in decorating is as wide as that of the flower garden, from the palest flesh tones of roses, through the crisp pinks of sweet peas and carnations, to the blue-pinks of foxglove and mallow, and the brighter fuchsias. Pale pink, either a clear shade or dusted with grey, adds warmth to a room without being overpowering. Pinks are often the backdrop to a mix of red and pink on floral printed cottons, producing a pretty effect that nevertheless needs careful planning and restraint to prevent a sugary, overdone result. This is the quintessential colour scheme of the chintz style – the heat of red and the tempering calm of pink associated with an English summer garden.

ABOVE Subdued, earthy pinks and reds are clearly inspired by the fruits of autumn. The colour effect is rich and luxurious.

RIGHT Rich, pinky red walls are intensified by the furnishings in this sitting room. A battered leather armchair and kilim cushion cover highlight the reds, and plenty of glossy black in the fireplace and ornaments adds drama.

LEFT A stunning delphinium blue is painted in a thick matt finish onto the walls of a cottage. The blue has a warm, reddish tinge that makes it bright rather than cold, and it is highlighted by quantities of white.

RIGHT Experiments for a predominantly blue floral decorating scheme include touches of pink and mauve, which will ensure that the end result has colour warmth.

BELOW The inspiration for the decorating scheme on the left is to be found in delicate, intensely blue garden delphiniums.

blue, purple and mauve

The checklist of blue and purple names is powerfully evocative of the intense and unique shades found in this part of nature's spectrum: periwinkle, bluebell, delphinium, hyacinth, gentian and cornflower describe a range of blues, while lilac, lavender, heather, violet, damson, plum, mulberry, grape and aubergine take us from mauve to dark purple.

The colour blue was a precious commodity in ancient times. Its most intense and brilliant shade, ultramarine, was obtained by grinding down the semi-precious stone lapis lazuli, but this was so expensive that it was used only in paintings and by the Church. A bright sky blue was derived from the copper carbonate azurite. The most powerful plant source of blue has always been the leaf of the indigo plant, which when soaked and heated pursues its own alchemy by turning yellowish green before its final oxidization into a deep indigo blue. In Europe, the most common plant pigment was woad, but this produced a far weaker and less successful blue than indigo. Prussian blue, a ferric-ferrocyanide compound, was discovered in the early 18th century, providing a much cheaper alternative to ultramarine. Cobalt blue and cerulean blue – compounds made from the mineral cobalt with aluminium oxide and tin oxide respectively – were developed in the early 19th century.

Although technically a cold colour that appears to 'recede' from the eye, thereby making a space seem larger, blue used in decorating can be warmly tinged with pink or purple or have a jewel-like brilliance that feels anything but chilly. Most of the blues found in flowers, unlike the cooler sky blues, have this warm quality. Periwinkle and delphinium seem to have an underlying red, while the springtime colours of hyacinth and bluebell have a pink content that softens them. Painted on the walls, any of these flower colours will have a gentleness and depth that can be very compelling. Blues combine well with pinks or contrast cheerfully with strong sunshine yellow. They can be toned with mauves or cooled down with off-white for a more formal effect.

Purple is the grandest and most mysterious of colours, a potent mix of the heat of red and the cold of blue. Its creation once entailed huge expense, the pigment being

LEFT A crocus flower shows how luminous mauve appears when highlighted with red and yellow.

RIGHT Lavender-coloured walls in a bathroom have enough blue in them to avoid looking sickly-sweet.

BELOW Paint samples in toning hyacinth colours contrast beautifully with the dark plum red of a painted Victorian plate.

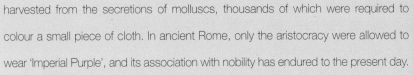

harvested from the secretions of molluscs, thousands of which were required to colour a small piece of cloth. In ancient Rome, only the aristocracy were allowed to wear 'Imperial Purple', and its association with nobility has endured to the present day.

The source of an affordable pigment that could be used to imitate the many purple shades of the flower garden remained elusive. Then, in 1856, the chance discovery of a purple synthetic dye opened up new possibilities. The colour became all the rage and was seen everywhere in fashionable dress and interior decoration. The new shade was named 'mauve', the French word for the stem of the wild mallow plant. Ever since its discovery, mauve has been a controversial colour. Some find it restful, almost ethereal, as a wall colour for living rooms or bedrooms; while others are repelled by mauve shades, which they perceive as sickly and somehow unreliable. As a result, the colour goes in and out of fashion with a vengeance. By 1926, Basil Ionides was certainly glad to see the back of it:

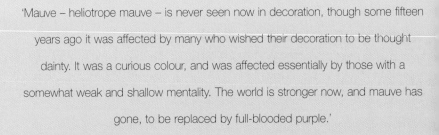

'Mauve – heliotrope mauve – is never seen now in decoration, though some fifteen years ago it was affected by many who wished their decoration to be thought dainty. It was a curious colour, and was affected essentially by those with a somewhat weak and shallow mentality. The world is stronger now, and mauve has gone, to be replaced by full-blooded purple.'

Perhaps we have gone weak again, because mauve is back in fashion. Or maybe, rather than shallowness, mauve reflects sensibilities at times of change. Just as it provides a visual link, a transition, between blue and red blooms in the flower garden, perhaps it is a natural colour choice at the turn of a century. It does need to be treated with care. Whereas in the garden mauve harmonizes with quantities of green foliage to become part of a soft background, the colour appears to make a much stronger statement when painted onto an interior wall. Yet when a mauve decorating scheme works well, with accents of, say, purple-red and clear blue, it is inspiring.

LEFT This deceptively simple decoration is, in fact, cleverly designed to make the best of the sunny lemon-yellow walls. Straw-coloured sisal flooring and pale-wood furniture temper the yellow's brightness, while the addition of a pinky-red patterned rug, fabric and ceramics ensures that the yellow stays upbeat, not murky.

BELOW Natural accents are found in lemons that are given an edge by their acid-green foliage. As a decorating combination, these colours work better under a strong tropical sun than in greyish, northern light.

yellow The natural language of yellow has to start with the sun and with gold, but then flowers take over when we seek to describe the intensity of the colour, from primrose through daffodil to buttercup. Fruits play their part, with banana and lemon; and then there are sand, mustard, saffron, sulphur, straw and canary.

Ochre – earth yellow – is derived from iron oxide, but more vivid yellow pigments have been sourced from a variety of plants found in different parts of the world. Fustic, weld, the bark of the quercitron tree, the barberry (berberis) plant, the South American annatto, the saffron stamens of crocuses, and simply crushed yellow berries have all been plundered for pigment. In the early 19th century the processing of chrome ore produced a bright and slightly acidic colour, chrome yellow, sparking fashions similar to those that were to take place upon the discovery of mauve – and a similar backlash.

Yellow is the colour that is closest to light, and because it seems to advance towards the eye, it makes a space seem smaller than it actually is. The acquisition of just the right shade of yellow in decorating is notoriously difficult. Very pale primrose yellows can sometimes end up looking too creamy and sickly, lemon yellow can be sharp and off-putting, and sunshine yellow is very powerful. Mustard yellow

can be heavy and murky, while pale sand shades can appear dingy. The solution is to combine yellow with other colours rather than try to achieve a one-colour scheme. Yellow with white will lift it out of any dullness and also relieve the brilliance of a strong buttercup shade. A bright daffodil yellow with periwinkle blue is a bold and traditional rural combination. An unusual trick these days, but one which was fashionable a hundred years or so ago, is to combine yellow with a pale, sugary pink, enough to keep it clear of any green tinge. It may sound a strange combination, but a herbaceous border gives ample demonstration of the cheerful effect of yellow and pink.

earth

In the 21st century, along with our desire for an ecologically honourable home environment – either in fact or at least in appearance – has come a fashion for the neutral colour tones of the bare landscape. The phrase 'earth colours' might once have had a less than attractive ring, but is now a familiar label representing good taste and due regard for the environment.

The names of neutral colours from the brown/beige and grey/white spectrums make their derivation clear – peat, mud, mole, terracotta, coffee, bamboo, nutmeg, granite, stone, slate, pebble, charcoal, chocolate, chestnut, walnut, clove, cinnamon, fawn. In addition, the names of the original earth colours – ochre, sienna and umber – which were coined by the Romans to describe the pigments derived from soil, are also now widely familiar.

Iron oxide is the principal colour-producing agent in most earth pigments. Yellow ochre derives from clay permeated with hydrated iron oxide. Sienna, which is more reddish, is the result of a greater concentration of iron oxide in the soil. And umber, which is dark brown (its name comes from *umbra*, the Latin for 'shade'), is taken from soil containing manganese oxide. Burnt sienna and burnt umber, produced by roasting raw sienna and raw umber, are warmer and richer than the raw pigments.

Since antiquity, the earth has provided a range of yellow, orange, red and brown pigments that have been used by artists and decorators across the world, from Egypt and Greece to India and China. They were mixed in differing proportions to make other colours, such as grey and pink; then black and white were added to the available palette. The Egyptians made black from carbon and white from gypsum; in India black was derived from soot and white from gypsum, kaolin and lime. The Greeks used chalk to make white and charcoal to produce black.

ABOVE The colours and textures of the earth – yellow ochre and sienna in the autumn leaf and gradations of brown in a rough wooden bowl and coconut shell – are the inspiration for many contemporary, 'organic' decorating designs.

LEFT A rich sienna is washed across the walls here, not in a perfectly smooth finish but in a rough texture reminiscent of the soil from which the pigment is taken. Unpainted wood and earthenware, along with a throw woven from shades of undyed wool, enhance the earthy look of the room.

LEFT A combination of white, cream, beige and brown – all shades of one neutral colour – is used here to produce a light and gentle interior. The interest is added by a variety of shapes and textured materials rather than by splashes of additional colour.

RIGHT Willow harvested by a basket-weaver gives ample evidence of the lovely range of hues produced by just one species of tree. These subtle brown harmonies are the inspiration for room designs such as that on the left.

INSET RIGHT Painted eggshells highlight the colours and textures in a choice of fabrics in natural, rather than manmade, fibres.

wood and straw

A decade ago, few people would have considered a decorating scheme based on brown and beige to be either attractive or acceptable. There were still too many memories of the 1970s' fashion that deteriorated into millions of 'His and Her' brown and beige bath towels and sludgy-looking toasters ornamented with sprays of brown wheat ears. Back in the 1920s, however, brown had a higher status and was considered a fashionable and dignified decorating colour. Basil Ionides, for example, suggests a brown scheme for a 'simple little drawing room', in which the walls are in deep ivory with panels of glossy bronze-brown, the paper edged with a very narrow band of gold. The woodwork was to be a matching ivory, the ceiling a lighter ivory and the floor a deep bronze, softened with an old Turkey carpet. Curtains are suggested in deep bronze satin with gold cord edge and yellow linings, with inner curtains, next to the glass, in red artificial silk. Covers and cushions are dull and brighter reds, and suggested ornaments are red lustre, copper and cream-white earthenware. The result is an interesting combination of brown, red and yellow earth colours that would also have been entirely acceptable in ancient Rome – and is increasingly so again today.

We tend to combine our earthy decorating palettes with natural, textured materials in pale colours, such as sisal flooring, unbleached linen blinds, unpainted softwood furniture and willow baskets. The overall effect is light, tactile and so neutral in colour that some people declare 'texture is the new colour'.

Noticeably, contrasting schemes of smooth, highly polished dark woods and bright white paintwork are creeping into fashion, highlighted with accents of turquoise or purple. These accent colours look fresh and modern, although, interestingly, back in the 1920s Ionides was suggesting interior designs using a combination of aubergine and turquoise. Used now against a neutral background, this combination seems to encapsulate the opposing forces of environmental awareness and new technology – as seen, for example, in a turquoise computer sitting on a sun-bleached wooden table.

stone and shell The use of natural, rather than synthetic, materials in decorating and furnishing may also have refined our collective colour eye a little. Certainly, we seem more attuned to subtle gradations of colour or tone than we might have been before such a concentration on all things organic.

It is unlikely that our ancestors would have been happy to surround themselves with shades of grey and white and little else, but many a modern interior is subject to such colour austerity. The emphasis has shifted; whereas decorating manuals once concentrated on decorating, and on the colours and materials needed for the job, contemporary books about interiors often feature an altogether less practical approach and an imprecise vocabulary. The home is a place of healing in which we are encouraged to create a sympathetic environment, and room schemes are dubbed 'spiritual', 'energetic', 'breathing' and the like. Colour schemes are suggested in order to provide 'sanctuary' in a room, rather than their own drama. Such havens might well be created through the use of greys and white – gentle tones with gentle names, such as dove, pearl, silver, mouse, shell, magnolia, vanilla, opal and pebble. Gone is Ionides's strict maxim that grey should be used only as a background to display other objects and colours; now every shade of stone is admired for its own beauty.

RIGHT Walls painted in greenish grey and stone, white woodwork, a pale scrubbed brick floor and bleached wood are used to create an undemanding colour scheme for a hallway that seems to pull in the daylight.

BELOW Blue-grey and white squash demonstrate a beautiful, silvery colour palette that could be the natural inspiration for the hallway shown on the right.

LEFT An intense sky blue is dabbed onto the walls in this seaside house, producing something of the texture of the sky. A pinky white, the colour of the plaster base of a fresco, is used for the ceiling, and pale, unvarnished wooden floorboards and banisters add a neutral warmth.

RIGHT The inspiration for sky decorating colours is all around: it is seen here with unthreatening fluffy white clouds against a familiar blue.

sky

The qualities of light have long fascinated artists. The Impressionists, in particular, were obsessed with its accurate rendition; Claude Monet returned to his water lilies at different hours of the day to paint the effect the changing light had upon their colours and forms. The colours of the sky are those we associate most closely with light, with an airiness that is an attractive option for an interior. Generally pale, pastel and, if not actually blue, at least tinged with blue, these colours tend to carry names synonymous with the elements – sky blue, dawn pink, cloud, snow, ice white. In the early 19th century, there was a popular pastel shade named 'etherial blue', giving a strong indication of the sort of atmosphere it was intended to create in a room. Today, shades of paint colour with similar intended properties might be called 'aurora' or 'aura', or even have individual cloud-formation names, such as 'cumulus'.

Light sky blues can make a space appear larger than it actually is, because blue is a 'receding' colour that will trick the eye into believing that walls or ceilings are further away. This can be a huge advantage for rooms that are small or have little natural light, particularly if the blue is combined with off-white. It is also a popular decorating scheme for houses that are set in a wide or flat landscape and therefore seem to be crying out for a close relationship with a large sky. Wooden seaside houses, surrounded by the blues of sky and water, are often treated in this way; bright, floral or foliage colours would seem out of place in such an environment.

The danger with cool blue is that it becomes altogether too cold – so restful that it is enervating. A contemporary solution is to combine it with straw or sand colours for other surfaces and furnishings. Natural fibres such as seagrass or sisal can be used for flooring and richly coloured woods for furniture, so that the pale look is retained but warmed by the addition of elements of red and yellow.

A completely different feel is created by combining pastel blue and pastel pink, adopting the sky's palette of dawn on a summer's day. In order for the two shades

to harmonize well, the blue should have a touch of red or purple in the mix. Rooms decorated in this way acquire a gentle warmth and a real prettiness, with the sweetness restrained by the use of darker wood and upholstered furniture. There are variations on a theme: Basil Ionides suggests a Wedgwood blue sitting room in which the floor is 'black, with mauve Samarkand rugs'. Sky colours here take on an edge with the addition of black, and an Art Deco feel that was beginning its heyday when he was writing in 1926.

LEFT Several shades of cool sky blue are combined with a creamy off-white that tones with them; a pure white would set up an uncomfortable contrast. All over the room – in ceramics, textiles and fresh flowers – are accents of pale, pastel pink that keep the design warm.

BELOW Sky colours are mixed and ready for an interior design that will reflect a cool northern dawn – dusty pink, palest grey and off-white.

An extreme version of the decorating approach that utilizes pale sky colours is a scheme based entirely on the use of white. At its purest, white is an absence of colour, but many of the shades that we call white actually contain hints of other colours. The tiniest amount of red, blue, yellow, green, purple or orange gives white a different quality, and it is surprising just how many slightly different shades are possible.

An interior decorated with tones of white will, paradoxically, work well only if bright, pure white is avoided in the mixture. This is because bright, dazzling white throws up an immediate contrast – which is all well and good if that is the effect required, but when it is set against a mix of off-whites, it will make them appear muddy or even dirty. Further, it is best to stick to harmonizing, rather than contrasting, shades of off-white; that is, those tinged with similar and not opposing colours. Greenish white and greyish white will combine well; and creamy whites with elements of brown or yellow will look good together. Problems may arise, however, if a greenish white is put next to a pinkish white – suddenly a contrast appears between the two shades and the result looks dingy.

As we have seen, colour is the means by which we are able to distinguish form, so when there is very little colour in a decorating scheme, particular attention needs to be paid to the shapes and textures of the elements of a room. Surfaces that are all white would be almost impossible to distinguish if they were entirely smooth, so textured finishes are important to prevent them looking like an amorphous mass. Rough surfaces create contrasts between light and shadow, making objects distinguishable in schemes that speak a language purely of white.

ABOVE A white bathroom employs enough green- and gold-tinged shades of white to prevent the room from seeming cold. A further lift is achieved with the gold picture frame that emphasizes the colour content of the whites.

LEFT Clever white decorating exploits the textures of the fireplace, the weave and ironed folds of linen and even the chipped paint of an old toy boat. A beige-white paint is used on the walls at dado level, topped with a very pale yellow stripe that allows the different shades of white to be distinguished.

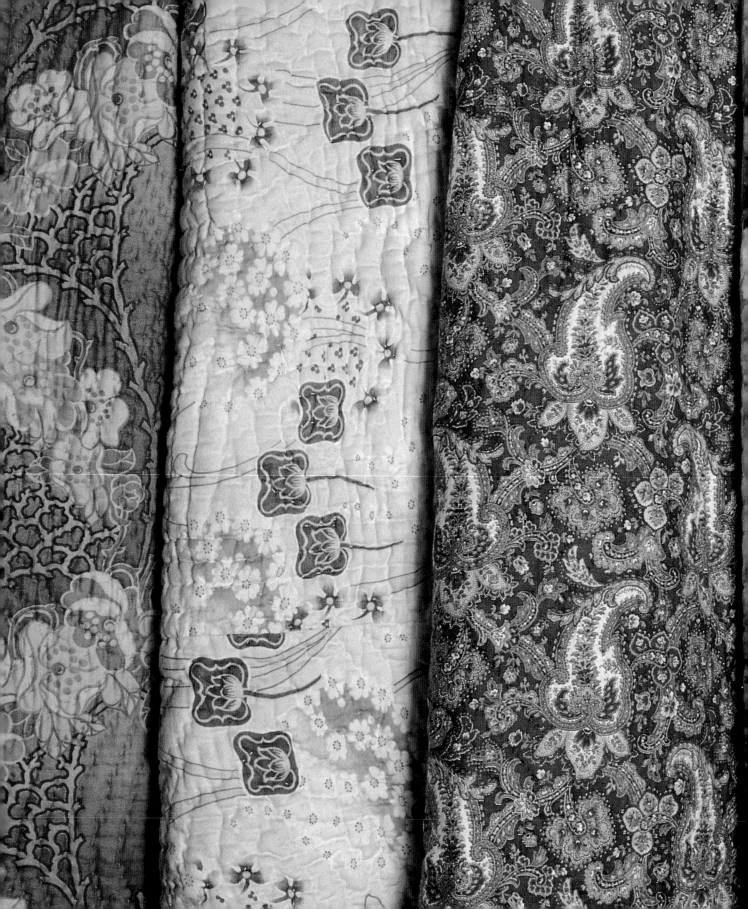

Textiles

PREVIOUS PAGES
Quilted chintzes in a
variety of floral designs,
both naturalistic and
stylized, are displayed
alongside each other.
The green and red
Indian fabric in the
centre uses the
Kashmiri *boteh* motif
from which paisley is
derived (see page 60).

LEFT Simple, stylized
flower sprays,
reminiscent of late 18th-
century textile designs,
are scattered over a
plain cream ground in
this covered screen.
The chair is upholstered
in a completely plain
cream, trimmed with
mother-of-pearl
buttons.

RIGHT Insects and
leaves are caught in
three-dimensional
weaves on a range of
contemporary fabrics.
Matt grounds set off
the shiny threads that
are used to imitate the
glossy exoskeletons of
the insect world and the
smooth surfaces of
leaves such as beech.

Just as the success of a garden depends, above all, on the effect that it achieves with texture, so too does the appeal of textiles. Combinations of shiny leaves and soft, velvety petals, or of rough bark and crumbling soil, give a garden softness, depth and drama. In interior design, textiles share similar qualities, with their surfaces that look and feel as varied as those of the natural world and that have the same softening effect. They are the ideal materials for art to employ in imitation of nature.

It is no coincidence that descriptions of pretty gardens or traditional meadows often speak of the ground being 'embroidered' with flowers, or that the backdrop of an embroiderer's work is itself called the 'ground'. In Elizabethan times, gardening and embroidery were seen as complementary arts, both accomplishments of the lady of an affluent house, and both requiring a similar attention to detail. An Elizabethan embroiderer used her own garden as inspiration for her textile designs, in which she not only represented but also improved upon the original – with perfect blooms and, sometimes, imaginary plants.

Whether the blooms of an English cottage garden are reproduced on printed chintz, or the formal geometry of a Persian garden finds its echo in the pattern of a carpet, textiles have been universally inspired by the natural world.

print

The skills of embroidery and weaving were laborious and time-consuming, and the quickest way in which to reproduce a pattern on a textile surface was to print it, using a woodblock that could repeat the motif over and over again. Fabric printing using fast dyes was known in ancient Egypt and China; for example, a printed lotus flower motif has been found on fragments of Egyptian textiles. Medieval European fabrics characteristically featured repeat patterns of circles or lozenges containing simple, stylized flowers such as daisies and fleurs-de-lis. Such woodblock prints, often in black ink on a coloured ground, were cheap substitutes for expensive woven silks and brocades.

The Western market for printed textiles really exploded with the importation of Indian printed calicoes in the 17th century. The technology of colour dyes was unsophisticated in the West, resulting in dull shades, but here were brilliant dye-fast

LEFT, BELOW AND RIGHT The lilac tree has been a cultivated plant of European gardens since the 16th century – a history that has ensured its habitual use as a decorative motif. The lilac chintzes used on the left for cushions and on the right for curtains are modern productions based on late 19th-century patterns. The lilac's soft mauves, purples and whites, combined with grey-green leaves, are the perfect vehicle for the muted, 'aged' garden chintzes that still remain fashionable in country-house decorating schemes. The tree's sinuous stems and drooping blooms lend themselves well to repeating the pattern over long lengths of fabric.

colours, produced by Eastern textile artists with a developed knowledge of the variety and strengths of mordants (metal salts) necessary to fix vegetable-dye colours into cloth. Bright reds, indigo blues, yellows and blacks dazzled a market that couldn't get enough of the miraculously economic cloth. The technology was quickly learned, and the printing of cotton in the Indian manner was established in Britain by the late 1600s.

chintz The resulting fashion in Europe for chintz (the word derived from the Hindu *chint*, meaning coloured or variegated), which was used in the 17th century for lavish bed and wall hangings, has lasted until the present day. Such has been its grip that a historian writing in 1935 declared: 'Truly chintz may be said to represent the feeling of the Englishman and his home as it really is.' Another commentator, writing at the same time, saw the craze less kindly, describing in withering terms the 'pitiless' decorative naturalism that has 'a fatal attraction for the British mind'.

BELOW This bedroom displays an astonishing range of printed floral fabrics inspired by different styles and periods. The patterns work well together because the colours have been limited to a palette of pink, blue and white. The bed is upholstered in a fabric that would not have looked amiss at the turn of the 18th century, while the curtains are a Victorian chintz pattern in full sway.

BELOW CENTRE The edible flowers of the herb borage have long been used to decorate salads, but they also provide inspiration for the simple printed cottons often used for soft furnishings and dresses.

BELOW RIGHT Before beginning to decorate a room such as the bedroom shown opposite, it is essential to have a clear idea of the colours – their varieties and shades – that will dictate the look. The inclusion of too many would bring chaos to a scheme so busy with pattern.

It is the Victorians who are most roundly accused of the excesses of naturalism in interior decoration. As the cities developed around the sites of industrial manufacture, nostalgia for the countryside (its poverty and rigours presumably forgotten) encouraged the style. Cottage garden flowers, in all their blowsy summer abundance, covered every available centimetre of chintz, leaving no background colour on which the eye could rest. Roses, hydrangeas, lilacs, hollyhocks, dahlias were reproduced as large as life – or even larger.

The overwhelming nature of these printed cloths was exacerbated by the use of the mineral and synthetic dyes that were developed in the 19th century, producing colours that were even brighter, such as acid greens and shocking pinks. Chrome yellow became all the rage in 1820, and mauve, famously discovered by William Perkin during experiments to synthesize quinine, was a completely new and wildly fashionable shade from the middle of the century.

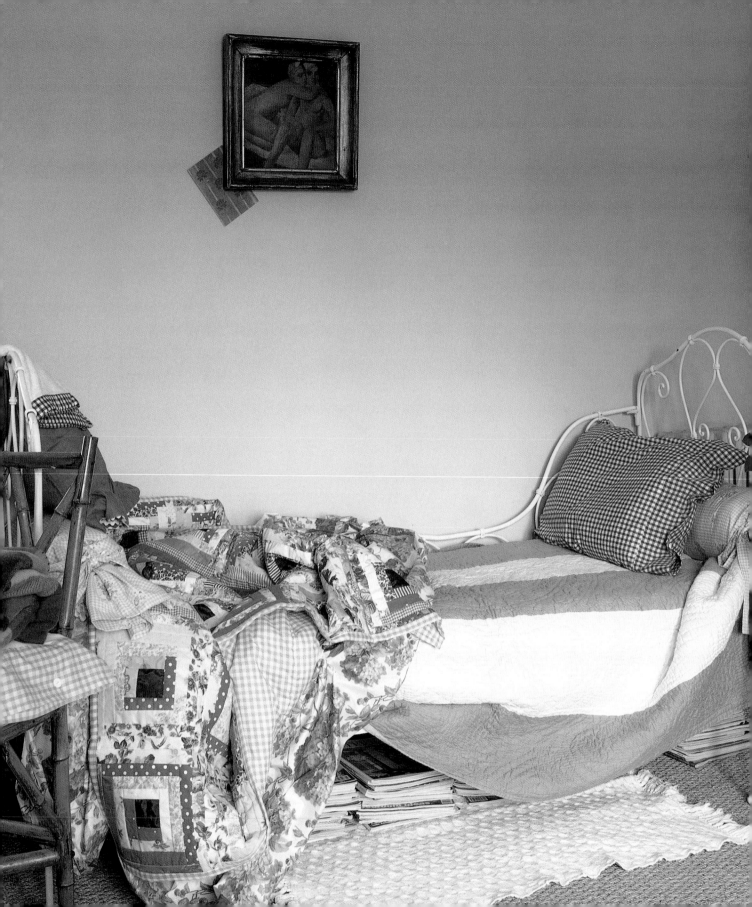

LEFT AND BELOW
Hydrangeas were introduced into Western gardens from China in the 18th century, and their popularity was established with the vogue for everything decoratively Chinese. On this bed, the quilt lies on a sheet decorated with hefty blue hydrangeas. The quilt itself is made up of a variety of printed cottons, some floral and others with geometric patterns. One of the beauties of working with chintzes is that if the colours relate well, all sorts of styles and patterns can be combined in this way.

Chintz patterns were not always so extravagant. They had absorbed a complex array of fashions and influences along the way. The early Indian imports, with their stylized Eastern flowers and trees, were not entirely to Western tastes, so Western traders shipped out patterns, many influenced by a taste for Chinese ornament, for the Indian craftsmen to imitate. They, of course, did so in Eastern style, producing their own interpretations of English florals. When these textiles reached China, the Chinese assumed that the flower motifs were Indian, and so it came full circle.

In France, toile de Jouy printed cottons, produced in Jouy-en-Josas, near Versailles, from 1770, depicted whole landscapes and stories in fine detail. Engraved onto copper plate and then printed in a single colour – usually red, blue, brownish-black or purple – on undyed calico, toile de Jouy fabrics told the stories of the seasons, of pastoral pleasures, of famous monuments, of mythology, and of current events such as the 18th-century excavations at Pompeii. Similar but less well-known monochrome toiles had been printed in Ireland and England since the 1750s.

RIGHT These samples of contemporary chintzes, all inspired by earlier patterns, are typical of the fabrics used in combination by quilt-makers. Some have small floral motifs, others larger flowers that leave little background colour.

The late 18th-century fashion for neo-classicism encouraged elegant and restrained designs, and a delight in being true to nature. The proliferation of printed botanical books known as herbals, with their hand-coloured engraved plates of fragile flowers offset by skeletal leaves, roots, ferns and even seaweed, further popularized the botanical approach. In the early 19th century, motifs were delicate and detailed, with small flowers drawn on a pale brown 'tea ground'; or they were designed in imitation of Chinese wallpaper. The 1830s saw more Eastern influence, and exotic striped tulips and carnations proliferated. Accompanying the 'Chinese taste' were rococo festoons and ribbons, which by the 1840s gave way to the bouquets and sprays of full-blown English garden flowers.

twentieth-century style

In the 1930s, what were then perceived as traditional English chintz designs – modest floral bouquets on faded tea-coloured backgrounds in the fashion of the early 19th century – were faithfully reproduced. Towards the end of the 20th century, a mixture of orientalism and impressionism influenced printed cotton designs, which favoured pastel colours, delicate flowers and pointillist patterns. Most recently, there has been a return to a crisp naturalism, a sort of new classicism that has more in common with late 18th-century tastes. Elements of the natural world – foliage, insects, organic forms – are reproduced on printed fabrics with striking realism and plenty of background colour and space. The patterns are gently repeating, instructive drawings of flora and fauna that are accurate rather than stylized. In a technological age, these garden motifs are precision-engineered.

LEFT AND ABOVE LEFT Artists have always been fascinated by the spectacular geometry of curling foliage and the abstract patterns that can be derived from them. This modern printed cotton uses ferns in botanical detail to produce a fresh, graphic design.

RIGHT AND FAR RIGHT Our ancestors did not view insects as undesirable creepy-crawlies, but rather as instructive fellow inhabitants of the natural world. Butterflies, decorating a modern silk here, are innately beautiful, but a medieval artist would have had equal respect for a lowly, industrious worm or an orderly bee.

pattern

From the comfort of our 21st-century homes, it is perhaps hard to imagine what life indoors would have been like in a cold climate five or six hundred years ago. Depending on the inhabitants' wealth, it would have been a question of earth or stone floors, windows with inadequate glass or no glass at all, few items of furniture and constant damp. The value of textiles – as hangings to offer protection from draughts and as coverings for seats, tables and walls – should not be underestimated. And, of course, textiles brought in colour, texture and pattern to excite the eye.

woven forms
Ever since the Middle Ages, European hand-woven tapestries have drawn direct inspiration from nature. During the Renaissance, wildernesses of foliage and fruiting trees were created in the French and Flemish

BELOW LEFT Studying the leaf-veining and colours of cabbages provides an insight into the effectiveness of woven textiles as a medium for designs drawn from nature. The similarity is not just in surface pattern, but also in the depth of colour and rich textural effects that nature and textile art both display.

BELOW CENTRE A rich, purple-red figured velvet is used for an irresistibly tactile cushion that is lavishly trimmed and tasselled. On the right of the picture is a cushion covered with a modern reproduction of a William Morris textile now called 'Vineleaf', showing the rich, natural dye colours that he once strove endlessly to perfect.

verdures, or 'garden' tapestries. In the French and Flemish tapestries known as *millefleurs*, landscape backgrounds to hunting or mythological scenes were studded with an implausible array of garden and wild flowers, animals, insects and birds. The flowers and foliage of these tapestries were stylized, and sometimes elaborated or wholly imagined.

The most gloriously prized woven textile was silk, first introduced to the West via the trade routes from China. Silk damask (in which the pattern is integral to the weave of the cloth) and silk brocade (in which the pattern, often appearing in gold or silk thread, is raised above the surface) have always been expensive fabrics. The depth of their weaves means that they can imitate the textures, as well as the forms, of living plants, and many of the most beautiful examples involve swathes of foliage and of round, full-petalled flowers. These fabrics are particularly tactile, taking on both the shape and the feel of the elements of the natural world that they use as decoration.

BELOW RIGHT The inspiration for the patterns of the richly figured textiles used on this bed is the tulip. Although the fabric design is in a Chinese style, the tulip originated in central Asia and became an enormously popular motif after enthusiasm for the flower reached fever pitch in Holland in the 1630s.

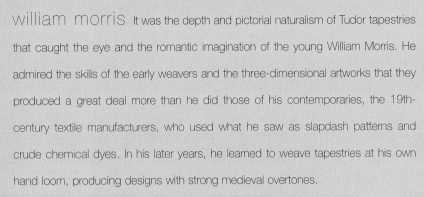

william morris
It was the depth and pictorial naturalism of Tudor tapestries that caught the eye and the romantic imagination of the young William Morris. He admired the skills of the early weavers and the three-dimensional artworks that they produced a great deal more than he did those of his contemporaries, the 19th-century textile manufacturers, who used what he saw as slapdash patterns and crude chemical dyes. In his later years, he learned to weave tapestries at his own hand loom, producing designs with strong medieval overtones.

Morris's studies of the art and craft of medieval designers, and of their approach to pattern on large areas of cloth, resulted in his development of textile patterns that were to have an enormous influence on future generations of designers. The solace he found in art was surpassed only by that he found in nature. His sinuous, organic plant patterns united art and nature with a depth of feeling that is evident whether or not you are a fan of Morris's designs. Here was stylization of the natural world achieved in the most fluid and resonant way in a celebration of English garden flowering plants.

The names of the hand-blocked chintzes Morris produced vividly evoke a spring or summer garden – Tulip, Marigold, Honeysuckle, Carnation, Iris, Rose and Thistle,

FAR LEFT Textiles here literally imitate nature, and very effectively, too. The colours, textures and sheen of these fabric poppies are entirely convincing.

LEFT The midsummer colours of apples exactly mirror those used in one of William Morris's most successful and enduring designs, Strawberry Thief. Designed in the 1880s, the original was a masterpiece of vegetable dyeing techniques, the result of Morris's complex experiments with indigo. The endearing pattern was inspired by thrushes reaching under the strawberry nets in the gardens of Kelmscott Manor, Morris's country home.

Jasmine Trail, Corncockle, Columbine. Behind the names there is, too, an evident nostalgia, a longing for an ideal world that was a far cry from the industrialized society of the 1870s and 1880s, when most of these textile designs were created. Morris was not a man of his scientific age.

indian styles

The Eastern interpretation of a garden was transcendental. The Indo-Islamic garden of the Mughal era was a paradisical retreat, where naturalism was secondary to an imagined perfection. The layout of the garden was orderly and symmetrical, constructed with a careful geometry complemented by the planting.

Indian textiles were characterized by simple, stylized floral motifs contained within geometric borders that echoed the tightly constructed, walled Indian garden. Stylized carnations, daisies, lilies, poppies and periwinkles decorated textiles from the 15th century onwards, and were augmented with an explosion of flowers during the reign of Shah Jahan in the mid-17th century. The arrival of new plants from Persia and central Asia – such as the tulip, iris and narcissus – and the accessibility of Western herbals in the royal libraries, provided Indian textile designers with a wealth of reference material for their floral designs. From these sources they interpreted real flowers and created totally fictional plants for decorative effect.

Perhaps the most familiar Indian motif is the *boteh*, the cone-shape in Kashmiri textiles (known in the west as paisley, after the Scottish town where the design was imitated). The origins of the *boteh* are mysterious: it may be based on a palmette leaf, fir cone, mango, teardrop or pear, or even the eternal flame of Zoroastrian iconography.

BELOW LEFT Sprays of unidentifiable (possibly fictitious) flowers are printed in blue, red and grey. The borders of the fabric contain the flowers like the walls of a formal garden.

BELOW CENTRE This cotton demonstrates the cross-cultural preferences that motivated the Indian textile trade. The flower motifs are predominantly roses, a favourite flower in the English market, but their style and the blue-and-white palette show Chinese influence.

RIGHT The large, formal flower sprays of this bedspread are styled to depict the essential shape of the flowers rather than draw them in elaborate botanical detail. The flowers are carnations, introduced to India from central Asia in the 16th century, and the indigenous Himalayan blue poppy.

BELOW RIGHT A simple daisy shape, particularly with many pointed petals, is often found as a motif on Indian textiles, perhaps because it comes ready-stylized.

decoration

The embroiderer's art applies an additional, textured layer to cloth, decorating the surface with an extra dimension. Long the preserve of the accomplished amateur as well as the professional, hand embroidered textiles are one-offs, original and unique works of the imagination.

From the 16th century onwards, there was a great appetite in Europe for newly discovered and imported flowers and their representation. Flower nurseries were established, luxurious books with botanical illustrations were published and the fashion for drawing, painting and embroidering flowers grew apace. In the year 1500 there were 200 cultivated plants in English gardens; by 1839 the number had soared to 18,000 as the plant hunters returned from all parts of the globe with their fashionable finds. By the 18th century, gardening was practised by members of every level of society, from the aristocrat to the humble cottager.

Embroidery over these centuries reflected the changing flower and fruit fads: for example, gillyflowers (pinks), which were all the rage in the early 17th century, were overtaken by tulips (rare bulbs were literally worth a fortune) and then auriculas. Fine exotic fruits, such as the pineapple, were a dominant motif in the 18th century; and roses, pelargoniums, dahlias and clematis came to the fore in the early 19th. Needlework motifs can be viewed like diary entries of the *arriviste* plants.

BELOW LEFT AND CENTRE These modern crewelwork designs are machine-made, but exactly imitate the colour combinations that would have been seen in the 17th century. One uses cream on a darker, heavy linen background; the other, colours that are in keeping with those that could have been produced using vegetable dyes. The flower and leaf motifs are heavily stylized, as much inventions of the designer as they are renditions of real plants.

RIGHT Embroidered and tapestry cushions in gentle pastel colours create the atmosphere of a timeless rural interior. A gentlewoman is at home here, drawing direct inspiration from the roses and summer bedding plants of her garden, and interpreting them in the subdued colour shades of a northern summer.

crewelwork By the 17th century, it could no longer be said that decorative flower and foliage motifs in Europe merely reflected indigenous plants and styles. Foreign plants and exotic garden or landscape designs were plundered for patterns in equal measure, and even had the edge with their novelty value. Meanwhile, the staple medium of 17th-century needleworkers in Europe and America was crewelwork. Crewel was an inexpensive yarn, made by closely twisting together long wool fibres, and it was embroidered onto sturdy cloths such as cotton twill and linen. Designs in undyed cream yarn remained popular (and suit contemporary tastes now), but were supplemented by patterns done in coloured yarns that could be used to exploit the full exoticism of their subject matter.

Charming stylized designs of climbing and twining flowering plants and trees clambered across the ground of the cloth. The unusual flowers and bold curling foliage of the crewelwork done in Europe, which was used predominantly on bed and wall hangings, were largely inspired by the painted and embroidered cloths imported from India at the time. The thickness of the woollen thread lent a naivety to the embroidery. Also, perhaps as a result, it gave the embroiderer artistic licence to move from real to imagined flora and to her own interpretation of plants gathered from distant lands.

appliqué The bolder the motif, the more stylized it inevitably becomes. Some of the most striking embroidery designs are those in which a cut-out fabric design is stitched onto another, larger textile. The origins of such appliqué, or applied work, are unclear. Certainly, appliquéd designs on cloth were done in ancient Egypt and in the ancient civilizations of Central and South America, and the technique was widely established in Europe by the Renaissance. In its widest interpretation, appliqué could encompass the sewing onto a ground fabric of all sorts of materials – gold and silver threads, feathers, quills and shells – as decoration, pulling the natural world straight into the interior of the home.

BELOW LEFT A rough linen cushion is an organic modern allusion to the lost wilderness of forest. The simplest leaf shape is appliquéd to the cover, designed to be stuffed full of woodland pot-pourri to enhance the illusion. Decorative wooden cut-outs of leaves are attached to its corners.

BELOW CENTRE This stunning piece of machine appliqué uses printed cottons with discreet textured patterns to make fresh green and autumnal brown oak leaves. The acorns are embroidered, as are the tiny flowers, beetles and worms that creep onto some of the oak leaves.

RIGHT A simple, contemporary appliqué design plays with leaf forms in white on a green background to produce a geometric pattern. The centres of the appliqué pieces have been cut out on occasion, allowing the backing material to show through. The cushion on the left has an ivy-leaf appliqué design.

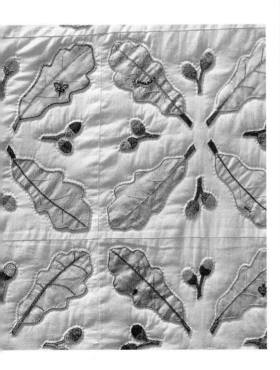

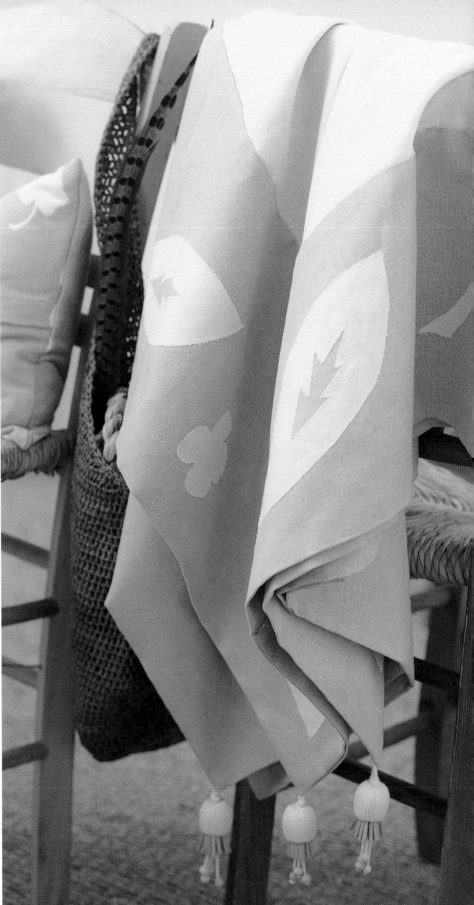

LEFT A wholly
contemporary piece of
whitework is used here
as a curtain. Twirling
chain-stitched stems
are given the simplest,
overlapping appliquéd
leaves, bordered by
fine lines of stitched
cutwork. A scalloped
edge completes a
design that contains
a combination of
centuries-old
embroidery techniques.

The natural shapes that lend themselves most readily to appliquéd designs are leaves. Their strong, often geometric outlines are easier to cut and apply than the delicate shapes of many-petalled flowers, and this embroidery medium has an abstract quality suited to such pattern. The simple outlines and unfussy shapes achieved with applied designs have encouraged a new interest in the technique in recent years. Devotees of modern, minimalist interiors rarely look kindly on elaborate floral fabrics and embroidery, but judiciously appliquéd leaves allow just a subdued hint of the natural world and find a way through the rigours of functionality. Some very pretty, gentle appliqué has been produced as a result. Sheer curtains, also very popular now to flutter in the breeze and diffuse the light, are decorated with airy white-on-white appliqué patterns. Undyed linen cloths and workaday denims, used for upholstery and cushions, are also to be found with self-coloured leaf appliqué.

cutwork The embroidery opposite of appliqué, cutwork is a design created by cutting away the fabric to leave a decorative hole. The hole is then either stitched around the sides or cross-hatched with threads to form a latticework design across its span. It has the appearance of lace, and cutwork was routinely employed in the 16th and 17th centuries as decoration for collars and cuffs. Again, the inspiration for the patterns is drawn largely from the natural world, with flower, leaf and fruit shapes juxtaposed to create repeating designs. Broderie anglaise, a type of cutwork in which small holes are edged with buttonhole stitches, was enormously popular in both Europe and America during the 19th century.

whitework In this type of embroidery, stitched patterns are embroidered in white thread upon a white ground. Versions of this technique, now usually machine-stitched, are also popular for contemporary textiles such as sheer curtains and bed and table linen. In this manner, plant motifs still find a way of creeping unawares into the starkest interior design plan.

LEFT ABOVE Snowdrops in pure white, with their delicate green-scalloped inner petals, have a lightness and brightness reminiscent of embroidered sheer white textiles.

LEFT BELOW Machine appliqué in a climbing leaf and branch design of white on white is used here for a shower curtain. Many textiles can now be treated with, or enclosed by, plastic to make them waterproof.

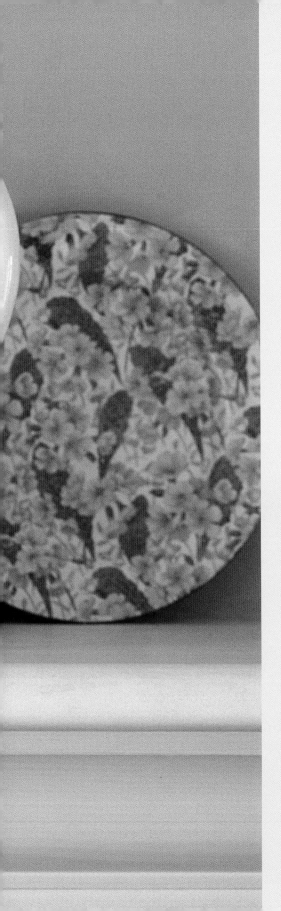

Ceramics and *Glass*

The making of pots reaches back to prehistory, and from the moment that mankind was able to decorate surfaces with scratched designs, the natural world provided inspiration. In the ancient Greek city-state of Corinth around the eighth century BC, pottery was decorated with stylized lotus and palmette ornament, in keeping with the Greek obsession with highly wrought foliage decoration. A century later in Mesopotamia, glass-makers were producing bowls with fluted edges in imitation of the petals of flowers. In China, ceramic skills had long been mastered, probably in advance of any other civilization. By the end of the 14th century AD, the Chinese were using all the available pre-industrial pottery techniques, and producing marvellously carved and decorated floral ceramics.

The desire to bring the prettiness of the flower garden or the wildness of the landscape inside the home is perhaps exhibited at its best – and, some would say, all too frequently at its saccharine worst – in the ornamentation of domestic ceramics and glassware. These materials are both sculptural and smooth, allowing either painted or printed surface decoration or moulding of the forms themselves into naturalistic shapes – or the two in combination. Naturalistic ceramic and glass decoration has over the centuries been restyled, borrowed from other civilizations, reworked, rejected and then resurrected again centuries later.

PREVIOUS PAGES Transfer-printed earthenware, with all-over floral designs of garden and wild flowers and sprigs of roses applied to moulded creamware, dates from the end of the 19th and first decades of the 20th centuries.

BELOW A modern china teacup and saucer are inspired by the delicacy of 18th-century English ceramic designs. The pink body colour on the saucer and classical border to the cup are embellished with a single transfer-printed camellia.

RIGHT A collection of 19th-century embossed earthenware includes a plate in the form of cabbage leaves and a jug with a large water lily in relief, perhaps inspired by Chinese ceramic designs featuring the lotus. The covered jar on the right is decorated with leaves depicting an acanthus motif.

BELOW Freehand gold-leaf designs of seedheads, a feather and a stylized bird decorate simple clear glassware. The designs are inspired by the delicacy of Oriental flower paintings.

traditional

Some everyday pieces of ceramic tableware that are manufactured in their thousands today are moulded in shapes and decorated with designs that date back hundreds of years. Our kitchens may have been redesigned with up-to-date technology and materials, yet many of us still serve our food on the same pretty plates that could have graced an 18th-century dining room.

blue-and-white china
The fashion for blue-and-white china has proved particularly indestructible. There are many possible reasons for its enduring appeal: cobalt blue is a lovely colour, particularly in combination with white; the designs seem to have taken on a mantle of permanent good taste; and blue contrasts well with food, which is rarely blue itself. But perhaps the real secret of blue-and-white's success lies in a more emotional response. Its patterns of gnarled blossoming trees, luscious peony blooms and Arcadian landscapes satisfy a nostalgia for an imagined and exotic past that is embedded in blue-and-white china's long history.

For a long time, white porcelain with cobalt blue underglaze decoration was the only type of Chinese porcelain known in Europe. The Chinese invented porcelain and the technique of underglaze painted decoration during the Yuan and early Ming dynasties of the 14th century, and huge amounts of blue-and-white porcelain were exported to Europe over the following centuries. In the 1600s, the new European fashion for drinking tea, coffee and chocolate also boosted the trade, so much so that porcelain from China was valued more highly than silver.

The interchange of naturalistic design motifs that is part of the story of chintz cotton (see page 50) also had a role to play in the history of blue-and-white china. European motifs were copied by the Chinese for their exports, and British manufacturers adapted the apricot and peach blossoms, chrysanthemums,

LEFT An elaborate Staffordshire covered tureen, looking for all the world Chinese, is decorated with the flora and fauna of an English garden. Old-fashioned roses in full bloom are visited by chaffinches, a much loved and common British garden bird. Moulded and then painted leaves are bunched up to form the knob at the top of the lid.

BELOW Antique English blue-and-white china is almost indistinguishable here from modern pieces produced in the same style. For example, the jug on the left of the top shelf was made by Minton in about 1820, whereas the sunflower design plate to the left of the central shelf is a pattern still in production by Spode today.

peonies, orchids and sacred lotus central to Chinese art of the period. In the late 18th century, the most famous English interpretation of Chinese landscape art appeared, in the form of the 'Willow' pattern. The design is thought to have been developed by Josiah Spode from a similar Chinese pattern known as 'Mandarin', and then engraved for Spode by Thomas Minton, fusing the existing European taste for the picturesque landscape with the concurrent fashion for all things Oriental.

By the 19th century, the cheap manufacture of transfer-printed blue-and-white ware allowed designs to loosen up, resulting in an extraordinary, albeit pretty, mishmash of patterns. Chinese motifs and those of European garden and wild flowers – drawn from nature and from books of botanical prints – were mixed together freely. In any case, many of the native flowers of China were by this time blooming in the gardens or conservatories of Victorian villas and being called English.

spongeware When making moulded earthenware, potters use small pieces of natural sponge dipped in water to dampen and smooth the clay over joins and imperfections in the hollow shapes. These same small sponges offer a cheap and

BELOW LEFT Roses, pansies and stylized leaves feature strongly on a selection of late 19th-century spongeware bowls. The farmyard pieces, featuring hens and cows, are the work of contemporary potteries.

BELOW CENTRE A spongeware plate, dating from about 1880, has a naive border of flowers planted in a row as in a child's picture. The central motif is an alert garden thrush framed by branches and leaves.

quick way of decorating the surfaces of the pots. The sponges can be cut or tied up into shapes, dipped in glaze colours and repeatedly applied to the surface, either directly or through a stencil, to make a simple pattern or all-over decoration. Sometimes hand-painted decoration is added.

Spongeware was popular from the late 18th century, particularly in the United States, where patterns were produced right up until the 1930s. The choice of shapes, with their stylized outlines, has traditionally come directly from nature. Daisies and roses, leaves and shells were widely used, while simple animal shapes – such as garden birds and butterflies and farmyard animals – often featured as a central motif.

The rough and vague outlines that resulted from sponging, and the limited palette of blue, green, red, brown and, more rarely, black and yellow denoted utilitarian pots that had no aspirations to high art. However, the naive charm and workaday honesty of the designs – and their apparent modernity – have made spongeware pieces collectors' items today, and have encouraged a revival of the decorative technique by today's craft potters.

BELOW RIGHT An enviable collection of 19th-century spongeware gives a good impression of the pottery's appeal. Creamy yellow glazes are enhanced by the earthy colours of their simple sponged motifs.

BELOW A collection of
transfer-printed and
hand-painted pottery
from various sources
has in common its
decoration with posies
of garden flowers. Some
are elaborated with
suitably sentimental
epithets or the names
of seaside resorts from
which they were bought
as souvenirs.

the victorian garden Gardening was a pursuit thought suitable for
Victorians of every rank. While the owners of bourgeois town villas cultivated their
geraniums, dahlias and clematis, they considered that gardening had a civilizing
effect on their poorer cottage neighbours, who in turn planted pinks, roses and
polyanthus. Everyone's garden was a little piece of paradise, a reassuring symbol
and a source of personal pride.

Fashion and snobbery affected gardens just as much as interiors. The question
of which flower varieties should be grown and whether their effect was tasteful was
debated in earnest by the late Victorians – and argument over colour and

ornamentation of gardens has raged ever since. A defensive essay in Sutton's
Amateur Guide and Spring Catalogue for 1881 comments:

'Those who rail against summer bedding make a fanciful entity called Fashion

responsible for what they deem low-toned folly; but we may conclude, without

violence to reason, that the prevalence of summer bedding indicates its usefulness

as a sort of visible antidote to the gloom we are so often involved in by our very

peculiar climate.'

The seed salesman had no cause for concern, and neither did the pottery
manufacturer – the popular market for garden flowers outside and for their
decorative representations on both table and decorative wares inside the home
was to remain secure for decades to come.

LEFT Here, the
chocolate-box design
is on a Victorian plate,
with idealized garden
flowers blooming
together out of season,
all encircled by a wide
sugar-pink border. The
pattern has been
entirely painted
freehand. Even though
its design is not
particularly good, its
charm still penetrates.

fantastical

The wide sculptural and ornamental possibilities presented by ceramics and glass have often given way to design confusion and, sometimes, to design excess. The results, generally speaking, have been received with humour and enthusiasm by the market and with sour disapproval by the design pundits of the relevant age.

Unsurprisingly, many of the more wacky ornamental ideas applied to ceramics and glass appeared during the late 19th century, when populations clouded by industrial smoke and a fast-changing world wanted colour and fun and anything that reminded them of the idyllic rural life that they had never actually experienced. Their sentimentality was severely frowned upon by Charles Eastlake, the most influential British design commentator of his day. In a series of articles entitled 'Hints on Household Taste', published in *The Cornhill Magazine* in the 1860s, he had strong words about the artistic merit of motifs taken from nature and used in interior design:

'The *quasi*-fidelity with which the forms of a rose or a bunch of ribbons... can be reproduced on carpets, crockery, and wall-papers will always possess a certain kind of charm for the uneducated eye, just as the mimicry of natural sounds in music... will delight a vulgar ear. Both are ingenious, amusing, attractive for the moment, but neither lie within the legitimate province of art.'

In his hints on 'crockery', Eastlake became particularly censorious, finding that 'strictly pictorial representations of nature are quite unsuitable to the true conditions of design in ceramic art'. Furthermore, the ceramic colours and shapes were contemptible. 'The *quality* of colour applied in the decoration of modern china is generally bad,' he railed. As for shape: 'A simple ring or round knob would be an infinitely better handle for dish-covers, &c., than the twisted stalks, gilt acorns, sea-shells, and other silly inventions.' But it seems that few among the pottery manufacturers or the public were listening to him.

chintz china The floral china that is now dubbed 'chintz' china must have had an apoplectic Eastlake throwing plates at the wall. All the flowers in the garden, many in 'pinks, mauves, magentas' – the new, 'unnatural' colours produced by synthetic chemical dyes – that he so loathed, splattered their way across the whole surface of the pottery, often leaving no breathing space of ground colour at all.

These wares were the opposite of the design restraint and fitness that Eastlake so desired. Needless to say, the public at home and in the export markets loved them. As colour transfer printing developed, the chintz designs become cheaper, more garish and even more wildly popular. They were produced up until World War II, particularly by firms such as Crown Ducal, Crown Devon and Royal Winton. Crown Devon's pattern names left the design derivation – the flower garden – in no doubt: Azalea, Daisy, Fern, Marigold, Blossom, Nasturtium, Rose, Wisteria. Royal Winton either named its patterns after the flowers they depicted or gave them suitably romantic girls' names, such as Joyce-Lynn and Florence.

Today, chintz china is prized and collected, a symbol of the escapism of the decades, including those that witnessed two World Wars, when it was produced and enjoyed. Its enduring popularity is perhaps proof that we still imagine a garden of paradise on a floral plate or in a herbaceous cup and saucer.

BELOW LEFT In the late 19th century, the pottery industry was celebrating advances in the technology of transfer printing polychrome designs onto its stocks of 'whiteware'. All the colours of the flower border, in their original haphazard mix, found their way onto new table services.

BELOW CENTRE Peony heads float in a bowl with a more restrained and sophisticated pattern that owes its inspiration to a mid-19th-century vogue for Oriental ceramic designs.

BELOW RIGHT Collections of Victorian non-matching china with overall, transfer-printed designs work well. The exaggerated nature of the designs is emphasized by pulling them together in medley.

RIGHT Floral designs were more widely used for tea services than for dinner services, as the style was deemed appropriate to the genteel nature of what was once a regular meal. The cups and saucers seen on the right date from the 1920s, when the use of colour and pattern became a little more restrained.

LEFT AND BELOW
A contemporary plate, embossed in a pattern of overlapping leaves, is finished with a thick and lustrous green glaze. Inspiration for such ceramics has been drawn from the vegetable garden since the 18th century.

relief ware

A very different aspect of nature was depicted in the high-relief pottery of the 16th-century ceramicist Bernard Palissy. A French 'Renaissance man' who took ceramic realism to an extreme, Palissy was a scientist and philosopher as well as a ceramic artist. He became fascinated by the development of polychrome ceramic glazes, particularly those that imitated the graduated hues of the natural world, and used his pioneering glazes on an extraordinary range of moulded, largely decorative pottery, often in the form of large platters and dishes. The moulds were glimpses of teeming nature – areas of ground curling with plants, strewn with leaves and inhabited by creatures of the forest floor or by pond or sea life.

The development of his art led him into a brutal naturalism. He began by creating ceramic moulds from actual natural elements, such as acorns, shells or strawberries, and then developed his art by killing and casting the living creatures that he wanted to reproduce exactly in clay – snakes, lizards, fishes, frogs, slow worms and the like. Though he was famous in his time (he was brought to work in Paris in 1566 by the queen of France, Catherine de' Medici), his methods were later much criticized, with commentators declaring that he could not be an artist as he was obviously incapable of actually sculpting the animal forms. Scientifically, he was well ahead of his time; it was not until 250 years later that another French potter, Charles-Jean Avisseau, discovered the lost secrets of Palissy's work and sparked a revival of this ceramic form. In the second half of the 19th century, moulded plates of fish and langoustines, fantastical grottoes and vases shaped like trunks of trees with snakes climbing them became fashionable again. Known as Palissy Ware, these pieces are collected and valuable, and are now also reproduced industrially.

fruit and vegetables

Exotic fruits brought to the West by plant hunters had enormous social cachet. Pre-eminent among them was the pineapple, native to South America and notoriously difficult to cultivate in temperate climes. Although Christopher Columbus tasted the fruit at the end of the 15th century, it was nearly

LEFT AND BELOW
The perfectly circular shape of the sunflower lends itself well to a motif for a plate. The cross-hatching of its central seed case is stylized with a geometry that is offset by a slight irregularity in the surrounding petals. The most spectacular of the daisy-like flowers, the sunflower was a favourite motif of the late 19th-century Aesthetic movement.

200 years before it was successfully grown in Europe. Rich 18th-century households set teams of gardeners to work to grow the fruit in glasshouses so that it could tickle the taste buds of honoured guests – and make clear how affluent and cultured were their hosts.

The pineapple's fabulous shape also made it a wonderful spiky centrepiece for the exotic table settings of the 18th century, and, of course, its decorative potential did not go unnoticed by artists and craftsmen. Pineapples began to appear carved in wood or stone at the top of grand gateposts, were sculpted in relief on architectural facades, were featured in textiles and wallpapers and were realized in ceramic. A pineapple-shaped and glazed teapot was an item of high fashion. And pineapples were not the only 18th-century ceramic models; a teapot might be in the shape of a cauliflower or a cabbage, and a jug might be formed from leaves. By the middle of the century, moulded leaf tableware and decorative pieces were made in large quantities.

novelty ware Pottery manufacturers in the 1920s and 1930s, caught in the grip of producing novelty ware to capture a market during the Depression, re-sparked a fashion for moulded ornamental wares, adding a whole garden of floral patterns. The Stoke-on-Trent pottery Wiltshaw & Robinson had specialized in ornamental wares since the 1890s, and from 1925 began to make novelty earthenware for the table. By 1926, a marmalade pot shaped like an orange sat on a leaf-shaped saucer; then a range of salad ware, shaped as lettuce leaves and garnished with tomatoes, was painted with brilliant-coloured glazes.

These were followed by moulded flowers such as 'Apple Blossom' and 'Pink Buttercup', the latter similar in conception to peony-shaped pieces that had been made back in the 18th century.

Other potteries that produced this type of ceramic included S. Fielding & Company, makers of Crown Devon, who moulded tableware in the shapes of poppies, pansies and snapdragons, then went the whole hog with wares in the shapes of flower-decked cottages, entire villages, windmills and inns. Beswick pottery succeeded in this arena with Cottage Ware, introduced in 1934 and now the height of collectable chic. The company's Sundial Ware concentrated on the English cottage garden, complete with standard roses and hollyhocks.

The fashion for relief ceramics never completely disappeared, and today both studio potters and industrial manufacturers produce such wares. Some are of very high quality, with luminous polychrome colours reminiscent of the Renaissance workshops in Florence of the brilliant della Robbia family, while others are in a tradition of unashamed novelty kitsch.

LEFT China flower posies were favourite Victorian confections, designed as jewellery and as ornamental pieces, and continued to be popular into the mid-20th century. This bouquet features well-loved garden flowers – rose, pansy, anemone and daisy.

RIGHT The handle of a creamware mug, dating from 1790, is beautifully sculpted as plant stems, finished with a modest daisy and leaf shape at the join to the hollowware.

pressed glass Glassware with relief patterns became available to the mass market from the early 19th century. Developed in the United States and taken up in Europe shortly afterwards, the technique of press-moulding, also known as mould-pressing, involved pouring molten glass into a mould and then putting it under pressure with a plunger.

Initially, manufacturers used this method to mass-produce the elaborate effects of expensive cut glass. But the moulded surface patterns of pressed glass were less sharply defined, and the material itself thicker, so the overall appearance suffered as a result of its imitation of a different art. At any rate, cut-glass patterns themselves began to be regarded as 'vulgar' by the late 19th century. The influential Victorian author and art critic John Ruskin thought the process of cutting glass barbarous, 'for cutting conceals its ductility and confounds it with crystal'. While design pundits encouraged the manufacture of pressed glass 'purely in accordance with function and formal appearance', once again the market absorbed the less refined, moulded wares based on cut-glass designs in which 'aesthetic appeal suffers badly'.

BELOW LEFT A pressed-glass fruit dish has relatively modest decoration, relying on its shape – like an open summer flower – for effect. The wine glass has more conventional pressed motifs in imitation of cut glass.

Gradually, however, pressed glass became recognized as a technique in its own right. Glass manufacturers produced elaborate tableware with fluted petal rims and moulded flower and leaf patterns, and the American 'lacy' glass had floral decoration on intricate stippled backgrounds resembling lace. Commemorative ware was popular in Britain, often featuring wheat, vines, grapes and other fruits in the decoration.

An increasing range of colours was added to the body of pressed glass. All manner of effects were developed, including coloured streaks, opalescent white and imitation marble. One of the most collectable types of pressed glass is 'carnival' glass, produced in the early 20th century by several American companies. Its name derived from the fact that it was given as prizes at carnivals. The brightly coloured pressed glass was exposed to sprays and gases of metallic oxides which coated the surface and, when refired, created iridescent rainbow patterns on the glass. The shapes created for carnival glass were largely organic, such as flowers and shells, and pressed indentations featured feathers, sinuous flowers and fruits.

BELOW CENTRE Victorian pressed-glass plates are inspired both in shape and surface pattern by flowers, and are wholly suited to an English strawberry tea.

BELOW RIGHT A fruit dish, used here as a rose bowl, has a geometric pressed pattern of rows of simple daisies, separated by a Greek-key classical frieze.

modern

Ceramic designers of the 20th century had thousands of years of ceramic history from which to draw ideas and working methods. Advances in technology, particularly in the 19th century, meant that almost anything was possible for surface decoration and glaze colours. Fashion also diversified, particularly in the second half of the 20th century, so that one person's taste for the antique and elaborate coexisted happily with another's preference for the modern and understated. This has given designers a freedom of expression and style that has sometimes had exciting results.

art deco This catch-all phrase manages to encompass not only the fanciful tableware designs produced in Britain from the 1920s until the start of World War II, but also the stark and simple pieces that originated in other parts of Europe and in the United States. Some British pottery manufacturers took seriously the geometric shapes and restrained, graphic patterns characteristic of pure Art Deco style, while others used the disguise of modernism to create ceramic designs that were really a law unto themselves.

The best-known English designer of industrially manufactured table and ornamental ware of this period was Clarice Cliff. Her hand-painted patterns on either conventionally shaped or fashionably angular pots glow with original ideas and striking chemical colours. Highly stylized garden flowers and landscapes were motifs commonly employed by Cliff on her famous 'Bizarre' wares, in as large a number as her purely geometric, 'cubist' designs. Perhaps her most successful fusion of the

LEFT AND RIGHT In the mid-1930s, the Stoke-on-Trent pottery firm of Wiltshaw & Robinson produced a number of floral embossed wares for its Carlton Ware range. One such was this 'Foxglove' design, in which the leaves of the plant are used to make the shape of the cup and saucer and a spray of the flower is employed as decoration. Tall garden flowers used as motifs had the obvious bonus of reaching up the body of the taller hollowware, such as jugs and teapots, as though they were simply growing there.

natural world with 'cubist' design was the pattern 'Melon', the round form of the fruit being the perfect vehicle for the style.

Cliff chose flowers appropriate to the brilliance of the scarlet, canary yellow, orange and bright blue ceramic paints: nasturtiums, crocuses, Canterbury bells, anemones, poppies, daffodils, delphiniums, pansies, petunias. The naive charm of these bright garden blooms was brilliantly captured in Cliff's work, particularly with the poisonous metallic oxide paints that are banned today but have an intensity of colour that is difficult to produce by other means. The vividness of the flowers, rather than their botanical detail, is what dazzles the eye.

Some British potteries of the time used a similar decorative approach to that of Clarice Cliff, employing brightness and stylized lines to reinterpret floral motifs. Others, however, remained attached to a more conventional, naturalistic interpretation of the English garden and its flowers. Although such patterns were often used to decorate conventional ceramic pieces, they were also sometimes applied to the new geometric shapes, setting up a strange clash of styles. They have their charm today,

LEFT This modern French coffee cup and saucer have applied decoration which is so convincingly naturalistic that it appears as though a few twigs of birch have been pasted onto the outside of the cup. Fine gold lining around the rims and a pale blue ground colour give the piece a light and airy charm.

the bunches of pink roses on triangular-shaped vases – most poignantly, perhaps, as symbols of English restraint trying hard to adapt to the new – but they are a part of a strange design episode, and very collectable now as a result.

A few of the finest ceramic designers of the age managed successfully to modernize the English garden theme. Eric Ravilious, the brilliant war artist, designed beautiful wares for Wedgwood from the mid-1930s. His patterns 'Garden', 'Afternoon Tea' and 'Garden Implements' used simple lines and a restrained sepia colour that brought the English garden motif bang into the 20th century. Among the pieces on which the patterns appeared were, appropriately, lemonade sets – earthenware beakers and a jug – designed for use on a sunlit lawn in midsummer, perhaps with a gentle game of lawn tennis or croquet echoing in the background.

contemporary naturalism After World War II, studio pottery in Britain was dominated by an austerity largely influenced by Bernard Leach, who, during the previous decades, had been producing undecorated, finely glazed pots

BELOW RIGHT It is not possible to get closer to the real thing than the decoration here. The impressions of autumn leaves are left bare in the surrounding glaze, as though they had just dropped onto the plates during a woodland picnic.

FAR RIGHT The organic influence at work in the design of these old plates might have been subliminal, but it is strongly accentuated by the mushrooms. The matt glazes and fluted edges of this basic earthenware make it look strikingly like edible fungi.

informed by his studies in Japan. Eventually there was something of a backlash against 'brown pots', so that by the 1970s and 1980s, influential designers were working with spattered coloured patterns and large, loose florals that owed some debt to the vogue for the paintings of the Impressionists.

More recently, ceramic design has looked beyond the garden fence to the uncultivated landscape that we now fear losing. Woodland trees and unsophisticated wild flowers, and the organic forms and colours of nature, are the images that we want around us inside our homes. Now that we have (or imagine that we have) nature too much under control, we perhaps want to be reminded of nature in the raw, no longer feeling the need to retreat from its uncertainties into a safe haven, as our ancestors did. The enclosed 21st-century garden is not so much a fantastical floral paradise as another room of the home, and so we go further afield to satisfy a desire for rampant nature.

Some ceramic designers are interested in applied motifs taken from nature – perhaps just a scattering of leaves – while others are attracted to the shapes created in the natural world. These may be the textures of stone, bark or fungi reproduced on the surface of ceramics, or they may be the patterns that repeat in nature: the grain of tree trunks; the spirals of shells, ferns and ammonites; the explosion of a dandelion clock. There is certainly something a little less domineering in 21st-century ceramic designs inspired by nature than in those created in the previous century. They have a carefully thought-out naivety that seems to show more respect for the natural environment that is their inspiration. Natural motifs are no longer contorted to suit an ideal in the mind of the designer, but are allowed to demonstrate their own consummate style.

LEFT AND BELOW The daisy was used decoratively by the ancients and has been featured continuously by designers ever since. In the 1960s it was adopted as a trademark motif by the British designer Mary Quant. Exactly the same simple daisy form as Quant's can be found decorating the walls of medieval cathedrals. A contemporary ceramicist here uses a more delicate, star-like daisy, reminiscent of wild wood-anemones or of the cultivated variety seen on the left.

coloured glass Because of its translucency, glass easily imitates the luminous colours of nature – the colours of water and sky, and of sunlight shining through leaves and petals. Paradoxically, before glass was clear in colour, it came in shades of green. As early glass manufacture was unable to remove iron traces in the silica, the end result was a distinctive pale green.

To produce coloured glass, minerals and metallic oxides are added during manufacture. In ancient Egypt copper was added to make turquoise – a favourite colour in antiquity – and cobalt was used in 16th-century Bohemia to produce dark blue glass. A century later, Bohemian glass was coloured with gold chloride to produce a rich ruby colour. In 15th-century Venice, tin oxide was used to create a milky-white, opaque glass resembling porcelain, and 200 years later, calcified bones were added along with oxides to produce translucent white glass. In the 1800s, uranium was used in Bohemia to make a greenish yellow, which, unfortunately, proved slightly radioactive. Also in that century, two new techniques in glass manufacture were invented: 'staining' (colouring the surface of the glass) and 'flashing' (coating clear glass with coloured glass and then firing to fuse the layers).

Decorative coloured glassware was at its finest in the remarkable hands of the French Art Nouveau designers Émile Gallé and René Lalique. Gallé's decoration included flowers and foliage, insects, and sea creatures. Lalique too used such natural motifs as dragonflies and flowers, beetles and peacocks. He was fascinated by the colour of moonstones, using them as inspiration for the opalescent pale blue that is characteristic of much of his work. During the same period, an American vogue for 'art glass' saw the invention of complex shaded colours. These became more refined in the work of American designer Louis Comfort Tiffany, who produced a spectacular array of coloured finishes. The United States remains the leader in contemporary glass design, and works in the medium are of great importance in the history of American decorative arts.

LEFT An engraved late 19th-century glass dessert stand glows with the colour of freshly picked raspberries.

RIGHT A collection of coloured glasses includes the apple greens that were once associated with early, iron-tinged glass manufacture.

BELOW A green glass decanter with silver mounts dates from about 1907, and a jug decorated with lily-of-the-valley sprays from about 1900.

Surfaces

PREVIOUS PAGES An imperfect, rustic style is maintained with unfinished surfaces: a faded stencil pattern painted onto the walls and a worn garden chair.

LEFT AND BELOW The garden plants and the wildlife of the local landscape of an English country house are reproduced with imaginative abandon in a living room wall painting. In order to encourage a naturalistic, *trompe l'oeil* effect, the painted leaves and tendrils of a vine reach beyond the walls to the paintwork of the door frame, as though they were alive and growing. The colours and abundant flora and fauna give the painting the feel of 15th-century decoration in which wild elements are stylized and tamed.

The very first introduction of flowers and foliage to a domestic surface was for functional reasons. In cold, damp and unsanitary rooms, floors were strewn with straw mixed with scented petals and herbs in an attempt to sweeten the unpleasant air. By Tudor times, scented flowers were used as nosegays in bedrooms, and tree boughs filled unused summer hearths. Perhaps inadvertently, flowers inside the home began to be cherished for their appearance as well as for their scent.

In the days when domestic houses contained very little in the way of furniture, soft furnishings or ornament, the walls, floors and ceilings were the only surfaces available for design and decoration. The desire to create pattern and visual interest in the home environment is irrepressible, even when it means working against the odds to improve the most basic situation. Medieval houses, for example, typically had mud floors – not the most promising decorative surface – but these were sometimes prepared with the addition of bones, which not only bound the mud together, but also could be arranged in pleasing patterns. In the 16th century, cottagers added interest to their mud floors using coloured sands; and in parts of India, mud floors, as well as the walls, are still regularly painted with narrative pattern.

Before there were affordable textile hangings or wallpapers, the easiest way to introduce pattern to a house was by painting it directly onto the walls. Excavated Roman villas pay ample testament to the skill of early fresco painters, who routinely incorporated garlands of flowers, fruits and formal garden features into their designs. In grand medieval houses, a popular device was to mark limewashed or plastered walls with a grid of lines imitating masonry and then to paint stylized flowers or foliage within the boxes. Such painted decoration became more and more elaborate, employing sprays of flowers and sinuous stems of leaves and, eventually, whole garden scenes on the walls. What was then the cheapest and only available option has become an expensive commodity today, but artists still work to commission, painting landscape and garden scenes, sometimes as *trompe l'oeil* deceptions, directly onto the surfaces of walls and ceilings.

wallpaper

Hand-woven tapestries made magnificent wall hangings, but they were extremely expensive and only accessible to wealthy households. In more humble homes painted cloth was used instead, and then, from the 15th century, paper, which initially was block-printed by hand. The first papers, perhaps inevitably, took their inspiration from textiles, with patterns imitative of embroidery and expensive fabrics like damask and lace. Those that copied embroidery patterns were often illustrated with a field of stylized flowers and repeat floral borders; imitation damask eventually resulted in a fashion for flock wallpapers, and lace patterns had an interesting graphic appearance of linked and geometric flowers.

The new wallpapers were extremely popular by the end of the 17th century, so much so that a tax was levied in Britain in 1712 on both the manufacturers of paper and the 'stainers' who decorated them. The papers, which were produced by stationers, could not be made in long lengths. The hangings were therefore made by gluing together sheets of paper to form a strip just under 30cm (1ft) wide. By the end of the 1700s, however, a dozen 54cm (22½in) wide sheets were being pasted together into strips 10.5 m (11½yd) long – the dimensions of which have determined the size of modern wallpaper rolls. The strips were laid out and decorated by printing from wooden blocks, stencilling by hand or, more rarely, freehand painting. These methods encouraged designs based on repeat patterns that were the size of a manageable block or stencil.

LEFT Samples of contemporary wallpapers show the enduring popularity of old floral designs. All employ garden flowers, such as pansy, lily-of-the-valley and sweet pea, as decoration. The paper at the top of the picture is a 19th-century pattern by the British designer C F A Voysey.

RIGHT A contemporary room is decorated in a French rococo design wallpaper featuring roses, ribbons, exotic birds and musical accoutrements. The single red colourway may imitate toile de Jouy fabric of the period.

Once established, wallpaper remained in vogue until well into the 20th century. It perhaps reached its fashionable height in the 19th century, when a huge variety of patterns and qualities of paper were produced throughout Europe and America. The century saw an infatuation with strongly patterned wallpaper designs, most featuring garden flowers in abundance.

floral pattern

Late 18th-century wallpaper designs moved away from the patterns derived from textiles that had dominated the early years of their production. The results were arrangements that were less stylized and formal and more naturalistic, with faithful reproductions of garden flowers and exotic plants. Books of botanical drawings provided examples to copy, and the flowers of wallpapers became more glorious than any real specimen. The interior garden that could be pasted onto the walls was an idealized version of the real thing, everything captured at the perfect moment of blossoming, never to decay. Nature was brought thoroughly under control in replica, and such papers were popular into the 19th century.

Many of the floral wallpaper designs that we now refer to as 'chintz' were indeed copied from the designs of chintz fabric, and by the middle of the 19th century these papers could be printed using new steam-powered machines. Some wallpapers coordinated with cotton fabrics for an integrated, if overbearing, scheme for a whole room – a style that has remained in vogue for 'country house' interiors. It is, however, no longer cutting-edge, and the majority of contemporary rooms eschew wallpaper in favour of plainly painted or paint-effect decoration. Every few years a revival of wide interest in wallpaper is heralded and then dies down in the wake of our fear of appearing vulgar with the introduction of naturalistic, even nostalgic, ornamentation.

design backlash

Our 19th-century forebears were, of course, accused of such vulgarity in their choice of wallpaper design. Criticisms came to a head in 1851 when the English wallpaper exhibits at London's Great Exhibition were viewed

ABOVE Samples of simple, stylized floral wallpapers are tried out alongside a striped fabric to be used for upholstery.

RIGHT The look created in this hallway is a kind of contemporary Tudor, underpinned by a daring red floral hand-blocked wallpaper. Plenty of natural light and smart cream woodwork make the heavy pattern possible.

as technically accomplished but aesthetically inferior to, particularly, French designs. Charles Eastlake, in his 1860s' 'Hints on Household Taste', put paid to the acceptability of English wallpapers of the previous decades that displayed 'a suggestion of landscape; sometimes a bit of ornamental gardening in impossible perspective; sometimes a group of foreign birds, repeated at regular intervals; but often a curious combination of those diverse elements of design, mixed up with huge flowers and creeping plants, meandering over the whole surface of the wall.' If plants had to meander, then they should do so in proper style, he insisted: 'The leaves of certain plants, when appropriately treated, become excellent decorative forms. Of these, ivy, maple, crowfoot, oak, and fig-leaves are well adapted for the purpose.'

Salvation came in the form of Eastlake's own designs and those of other reformers, who reintroduced a stylization of plant forms in reaction to these perceived naturalistic excesses. The trouble with the rescue attempt was largely twofold: firstly, the designs produced by the reformers harked back to medieval pattern-making and appeared flat and austere; and secondly, the designers also reverted to pre-industrial techniques, hand-blocking papers that were well beyond the purse of the ordinary householder.

The hand-blocked papers of William Morris need to be considered in the context of their expense and their appeal to an affluent and artistic, rather than general, market. Nevertheless, his designs have since been hugely influential, and a number are still in production. By the 1870s, his sinuous plant forms were a fabulous mix of the abstract and the natural, combining the best and avoiding the worst of both the fancy chintz designs and the stiff geometric patterns of the design reformers of the mid-century. Our perception of an English floral for the decorative arts is still intimately linked with Morris's interpretation of garden flowers, fruits and birds.

LEFT The acanthus leaf was a favourite motif of the Arts and Crafts movement, as in this 'Granville' wallpaper designed by J H Dearle, William Morris's workshop manager, in 1896. A hand-blocked version is available today from Sanderson.

RIGHT William Morris designed 'Chrysanthemum' in 1877 and the pattern is in production again today by Sanderson, shown here in a celadon and neutral colourway.

paint

Plain painted surfaces of walls, floors and ceilings can be quickly ornamented by the use of stencils to produce repeat pattern. A design can be scattered at random all over a surface, used to make stripes or a chequerboard, or restricted to a border pattern around a skirting or cornice, or at dado or picture-rail height.

Stencilling was used by most ancient civilizations, from China and Japan to ancient Egypt and Persia. In medieval Europe this versatile technique of cutting a template and painting through it was employed to decorate walls with heraldic and geometric motifs in a grid pattern. In the centuries that followed, it became an affordable method by which tapestries and wallpapers could be imitated. From the

BELOW In this cottage, the panelling is not hardwood that might be polished to a deep shine, but a rough softwood that has been painted a gentle cream. To add interest to the expanse of wall in the hallway and stairway, alternate boards have been decorated with a repeat stencil pattern of poppies, daisies and delicate foliage. The use of simple cottage garden flowers gives the right feel in this small rural home.

BELOW LEFT A floor
has been painted
freehand with sprigs of
daisies, scattered to
give a random effect.
The idea for the daisies
was taken from an early
19th-century textile
with similarly haphazard
flowers.

BELOW CENTRE AND
RIGHT These floor-
boards are painted on
the diagonal in a large
chequerboard design
that imitates terracotta
and stone floor tiles.
The stencilled border is
a highly stylized twig
and leaf design, taking
pelargonium leaves,
illustrated below right,
as inspiration.

late 18th century, stencilling was used on floors as a means of creating precise repeated patterns before carpet became affordable. Intricate designs copied the patterns of fashionable carpets to produce a kind of *trompe l'oeil* imitation of the more luxurious article. Stencilling was used extensively in 19th-century Swedish and American interior design, and the technique saw something of a revival at the end of the 20th century with a fashion for down-to-earth rustic interior styles. Cottage garden plants – flowers, fruit and vegetables – provided inspiration for the designs.

Although complex patterns are achievable, simple flowers, foliage and fruit lend themselves well to stencils, as their forms can be stylized into shapes that are easy to cut and to use. And because the painting technique used in stencilling is simple, naive patterns are particularly well suited to the medium.

pictures Perhaps the most straightforward way of introducing representations of the natural world to the interior is through pictures, in whatever medium, hung on the wall. Cultures throughout the world have their own traditions of painting gardens, or specimens from them, in which nature is often perfected to produce a vision of an ideal world. Persian miniatures and book illustrations, for example, captured blossoming trees and flowers in glowing and romanticized vein. In 17th-century Holland, artists reflected the prevailing passion for the tulip and other valuable flowers in highly accomplished still-lifes in which every detail, from the dew drops to the insects, was drawn with great accuracy. In Britain, portrait painters such as Gainsborough often featured aristocratic sitters against the backdrop of their landscaped estates, while generations of amateur watercolourists have painted their own or their favourite domestic flower gardens.

A choice of pictures of landscape, garden or flowers can be a very individual interpretation of the natural world. It may entail the perfection and accuracy of botanical prints; the impressionistic idea of the colour of poppies in a field or the play of light on water lilies on a lake; or something more naive and evocatively childlike. The choice may be a photograph of a real landscape or a fanciful idea of a non-existent garden paradise of imaginary blooms.

LEFT A painting of a vase of garden flowers on a kitchen table has been painted with a deliberate, two-dimensional naivety that gives each specimen charm and dignity.

BELOW LEFT The annual flowers in this watercolour are painted in an indistinct, higgledy-piggledy way, giving the same hazy appearance that they would create naturally in the border of a cottage garden.

BELOW CENTRE These botanical flower prints and their descriptions are given a surreal edge; they are pinned unframed onto a plain wall, and an empty frame is balanced around them on the mantelshelf.

BELOW RIGHT Here botanical prints are given a more conventional treatment – framed individually and hung in a regular double row across a bedroom wall.

texture

In the same way that textiles – and especially embroidery – have always been a good textured medium for interpretations of the natural world, so too have terracotta and encaustic tiles. They can achieve a three-dimensional effect either in the texture of the clay itself or by stamped-in pattern or raised relief. Medieval tiles of unglazed terracotta, for example, used motifs such as oak leaves and acorns as well as geometric and heraldic devices to produce pattern that was part of the exterior architecture of buildings.

In Britain and the United States, the most extensive use of decorative tiles on interior floors and walls was undoubtedly in the 19th century. There was a huge production of encaustic tiles with patterns formed by inlaid coloured clays used on floors and of colourfully glazed tiles for walls, fireplaces, the backs of washstands and so on. Most commercial tiles were designed anonymously, their makers taking inspiration from textbooks of pattern – such as the British designer Owen Jones's classic *Grammar of Ornament* of 1856. This

BELOW LEFT
Handmade earthenware tiles with rich glazes look marvellous here with hand-thrown pots produced by the same designer. The tiles show a variety of influences, with a Japanese fish on one, a heraldic creature on another and contemporary motifs on some. Their homage to nature is in their earthy colours, rather than their patterns.

provided motifs derived from a multitude of sources including classical, Islamic, Egyptian, Indian, Chinese, Gothic and Renaissance ornament. Many of these designs were based on leaves, flowers or fruit, usually stylized into simple forms.

At both the Great Exhibition in London in 1851 and the Centennial Exhibition in Philadelphia in 1876, there were extensive and stunning displays of decorated tiles, many with abstract flower designs. These found favour with the public, with design commentators – and with royalty. Queen Victoria was a great exponent of the tiles she saw on show, so critics praised her good taste and helped promote a fashion. Remarkably enough, even Charles Eastlake in his 'Hints on Household Taste' has only good words to say about contemporary tile design: 'This branch of art-manufacture is one of the most hopeful, in regard to taste, now carried on in this country. It has not only reached great technical perfection… but… it has gradually become a means of decoration which, for beauty of effect, durability, and cheapness, has scarcely a parallel.' For once, everyone was in agreement.

BELOW CENTRE The splashback of a Victorian washstand is decorated with relief-pressed glazed tiles typical of the period. The bright green background colour was very popular, and the motifs are of dainty pink roses.

BELOW RIGHT An Art Nouveau fire surround still has its original tiles. The stylized water lilies are inspired by Eastern lotus designs, and are garlanded in the Western manner with leaves.

The pretty 19th-century tiles that we recognize today, some in patterns that are still in production, were decorated in several different ways. In America, there was an extensive manufacture of hand-painted tiles. In Britain, hand-painting was limited to expensive art tiles produced by designers such as the Arts and Crafts ceramicist William de Morgan, whose inspiration came from the magnificent tiles produced in Persia and in Moorish Spain. Industrial manufacturers copied de Morgan's and other designers' patterns and reproduced them cheaply by transfer-prints in a number of colours. Some tiles had an additional pattern pressed in relief into the clay.

Beautiful Art Nouveau tiles with stylized flowers were hand-coloured with strong glazes that were separated by raised 'tube-lines' of clay piped onto the surface like icing on a cake. Many of the flower and leaf patterns were abstracted to the point where, when mounted together, the tiles formed a sinuous geometric grid of plant forms. Art Nouveau designers were influenced by Japanese art and tended to use

BELOW LEFT This modern exterior tile has been made and ornamented in a traditional way for use in restoration work. Its motif is antique: the acanthus leaf pattern was developed in ancient Greece and has appeared in architecture ever since, adapted and styled by various cultures.

exotic flowers in their designs – orchids, lilies, radiating sunflowers, for example. To avoid the overblown naturalism of earlier 19th-century designs, they depicted flowers as buds rather than in full and voluptuous bloom. Such designs on tiles were extremely successful, perhaps because the curvilinear, attenuated shapes worked well with the geometry of the squares.

oriental carpets

In 16th-century Europe a carpet from the East was such an exotic and valuable commodity that it would very rarely find its way onto the floor; it was more likely to have been used as a wall hanging or as a covering for a table. Oriental carpets remain valued items to this day and, uniquely, have never been out of fashion in the Western home.

Persian carpets are often designed in deliberate imitation of a garden. Just as the garden is divided into formal square plots separated by paths and surrounded by

BELOW RIGHT Another tile from the same pottery has been recast from an original 19th-century mould featuring the branch of an orange tree. The depth of the relief work is necessary on a tile that will be used on the exterior of a building and perhaps at a great height.

LEFT An antique Middle Eastern kilim imitates a formal garden. In the section of the rug shown here, a highly stylized and imaginary tree is surrounded by a flower border with, perhaps, a stream beyond, complete with abstract fish.

BELOW RIGHT Although this large flat-weave carpet is from the East, it is heavily influenced by Western tastes. Large red roses bloom in a naturalistic manner that is not typical of stylized Eastern pattern-making.

FAR RIGHT This carpet shows the lovely colours that result from the gradual fading of vegetable dyes. Flowers and sinuous foliage are scattered all over the ground of the work.

walls, so the ground of the carpet is bordered into distinct areas containing stylized plants. In India, the flower motif that dominated art during the Mughal period appears in many guises in carpet design. One large bloom might dominate a whole rug; a carpet might depict rows of trees and flowers; a geometry of latticework might be infilled with flowers or tree blossoms; or a carpet could be scattered all over with clusters of blossom. Sometimes the blooms of different plants all appear on one stem, and sometimes identification of flowers is impossible because the flowers are totally imaginary.

The carpets illustrated here are all flat-weaves, made of wool without the pile that comes from knotting and cutting the yarn. Collectively known today as kilims, these flat-weave rugs are made all over the Middle East and Central Asia, sometimes by nomadic peoples, for whom they are adaptable to many uses and are easy to fold up and transport. Many of the patterns found on contemporary kilims date back hundreds of years to the traditional manufacture of a particular area. Each handmade example is unique and contains the individual ideas of its weaver. Older kilims, made from wool coloured with vegetable dyes, fade to soft tones, while modern products dyed with chemical colours have a startling brilliance. In all but the most abstract, patterns of flowers and foliage create a dazzling meadow underfoot.

Ornament

The furniture, furnishings and everyday objects of a home – be they mirrors and lampshades or jugs and bowls – are first and foremost functional, but they also have a strong decorative potential. The ornamental opportunities for domestic items made in wood, glass or metal are limitless. Ornament is subject to changing and cyclical fashions – at one time plain and austere, at another chock-a-block with applied pattern.

The overriding inspiration for interior ornament has always been the natural world – its forms, colours and motifs. Many great designers have made detailed studies of nature in order to understand the pattern-making principles behind its beauties. For example, applied ornament in the form of flowers and foliage has been used from time immemorial: the ancient Egyptians stylized the papyrus and lotus; the ancient Greeks the acanthus and honeysuckle; and the Romans the acanthus, vine, olive and laurel. All of these plant forms are still routinely used today in one interpretation or another – not copied exactly from nature, but translated by the artist into a pleasing pattern. Other designers have studied the geometry underlying natural forms, examining everything from pollen grains to snowflakes under a microscope in order to understand the patterns and the irregularities that give natural forms their subtle balance.

Designers and commentators have also engaged in ongoing debate about the suitability of any ornamentation to the piece it is decorating. Most have agreed that function should dictate the design – a silver jug that looks attractive but spills liquid when pouring is a useless object. Some have thought that a piece should remain plain, others that its decoration should be integral to its shape, while some have seen it as a no-holds-barred opportunity for elaborate surface decoration. Happily, the result is a glorious range of ornamental styles for furnishing the home, created over the centuries and developing still.

PREVIOUS PAGES Ornamental pewter collected here is polished to a silvery sheen. The curvilinear shapes and embossed decoration are in the Art Nouveau style.

LEFT Bits and pieces of various light fittings clearly show the extent to which nature has inspired interior objects – both in form and in applied decoration.

BELOW The design for this wirework chair was based on a spider's web. The idea is brilliantly carried through into the arms and legs of the piece with arching threads in imitation of those that would attach a real web to supporting plants.

furniture

Furniture provides good examples of the different ways in which nature inspires decoration: a basic shape may be decorated with motifs from nature, or the piece may borrow its form from nature. For example, one chair might be stencilled with flowers, while another might have ball-and-claw feet, as though its legs were those of a large bird or mythical beast.

RIGHT This antique bedhead has been cut in a scallop shape like a gigantic shell, and is painted freehand with flowers and foliage, dominated by a botanically accurate carnation bloom.

painted furniture
The art of painting on wooden furniture was perfected by the ancient Egyptians, and has followed fashion and circumstance ever since. European styles of painting on wood have changed with the prevailing tastes. In the 17th century, lacquered pieces imported from the East, with the highly wrought floral decoration also seen on ceramics, sparked a craze that resulted in Western imitations. The lacquering technique became known as 'japanning'. In the 18th

BELOW An antique American rocking chair is painted in traditional Boston style with stylized flowers, foliage and fruits. With its primary colours and naive motifs, it has a cheerful charm.

BELOW A handsome painted wardrobe with elaborate neo-classical motifs is given added glamour with columns and friezes and quantities of gold.

century, furniture was painted specifically to coordinate with the decoration of a room – for example, with floral wallpaper. Venetian painted furniture in a light-hearted, rococo style had elaborate small floral patterns. Regency chairs designed by Hepplewhite had light, stylized floral pattern; while chairs designed for the Oriental-style rooms in George IV's fantastical Brighton Pavilion were painted in *trompe l'oeil* imitation of bamboo.

In Germany and Scandinavia, painted furniture developed in a more rustic style. A folk tradition of floral painted furniture in imitation of grander pieces was the keynote of decoration in 18th- and 19th-century country manors and farmhouses. The most frequently used motif was the scrolling acanthus leaf favoured by the ancient Greeks, which was sometimes elaborated with the addition of ornate blossoms.

A similar tradition developed in America, with a very eclectic mix of regional styles, harking back to the varied European roots of the early settlers. Furniture was made locally, then finished with painted or japanned pattern. In early 18th-century New England, for example, almost every domestic wooden article was painted.

Connecticut was the largest producer of painted furniture, developing a distinctive style of floral decoration for chests and chests-of-drawers. The background wood was sometimes stained red in imitation of more expensive walnut, and typical floral motifs included sinuous stems, vines, tulips and roses. From the early 19th century, so-called 'fancy chairs' were produced by Lambert Hitchcock of Connecticut. These Hitchcock chairs were usually painted black and then painted and stencilled with flower and fruit motifs in colours or gilt.

The influx of Germans to Pennsylvania between the mid-18th and mid-19th centuries resulted in boldly painted furniture dubbed Pennsylvania Dutch (a corruption of 'Deutsch'). The cheerful, peasant style of decoration, within which families devised their own characteristic designs, was predominantly floral. The most popular flower motifs were the rose, lilac, forget-me-not and tulip, often accompanied by hearts, trees of life or peacocks.

RIGHT A wonderful inlaid desk shows the art of marquetry at its best. Each of the flowers – mostly various tulip cultivars – is made up of tiny pieces of differently coloured woods to show the patterns and shadows of the blooms. The maker has given much thought to the scale and balance of decoration on a large piece of furniture.

WOOD The pre-eminent French Art Nouveau furniture designer Émile Gallé was concerned with the organic forms of nature, declaring that 'wooden furniture should follow the lines of vegetable growth'. His furniture thus took on the form of plants, the lines of the wood appearing as though they were growing like trees. This idea was taken to its limits by another Art Nouveau furniture designer, the Belgian architect Victor Horta, who used the roots of trees and plants as inspiration, so that his pieces really did appear to be growing straight from the floor. For example, a large, complex root system carved at the base of a piece of furniture, with climbing branches and tendrils above, gave the impression of towering fairy-tale trees in dark and forbidding forests.

Gallé was also instrumental in the revival of marquetry, a cabinetmaking technique by which patterns are formed using small pieces of differently coloured woods (or other materials, such as ivory, bone, horn, tortoiseshell or mother-of-pearl). These are either inlaid into the furniture or made up into a jigsaw veneer to be applied to it. Marquetry was particularly popular for continental furniture in the 17th century, with floral and bird designs imitating contemporary paintings. There was even a marquetry fashion as part of the William and Mary style in England, incorporating motifs derived from the abstract forms of seaweed. These were a celebration of the inherent colours, grains and textures of the various woods employed – sycamore, holly and pear on walnut, for example.

Wood is one of the few natural materials that are ready for instant working into functional or artistic shapes. It is no wonder, then, that artists and craftspeople have explored its numerous qualities to carve and construct furniture that follows wood's natural grain and form, producing interior objects that are intimately close to nature.

LEFT This wooden chair has no applied naturalistic decoration, but its curving arms and legs create an impression of the natural shapes of the branches of a tree.

BELOW A small hall chair in classical style is carved with vine and grape motifs, a favourite device of the ancient Romans. Although recognizable, the plant has been stylized as formal ornament.

LEFT Garlands and swags surround an antique French mirror, which reflects the outline of a gilded candelabra moulded in the form of a spray of flowers. Some of the flowerheads form holders for the candles.

BELOW LEFT Wrought iron shaped as rosebuds and foliage has, with age, developed a patina that makes its appearance even more naturalistic.

BELOW RIGHT As art imitates nature, the decorative purplish-green heads of eryngium look as though they might be made of metal.

light

Reflective materials like crystal, mirror glass and metals are highly prized for the extra light they bring into an interior and for their design versatility. Through the centuries, the bouncing of natural light, candlelight and, later, electric light off a shiny surface has made an enormous difference to the illumination of dark rooms. An added bonus is the effect of jewel-like richness inherent in the materials.

LEFT Nature's reflective inspiration is captured here in dewdrops shimmering on a leaf.

BELOW Although this picture might appear to be of tree branches caught up in an icy pond or dew on a leaf, it is, in fact, a contemporary chandelier made from pieces of broken glass and metal. Its designer says glass makes her think of water, and that the aim of her design is to create a swirl of flowing movement through the branches of the chandelier. It is lit by dozens of tiny halogen bulbs that produce a dappled spread of both light and shadow.

metalwork and mirrors

A carefully placed mirror can bring the outside directly into a room, reflecting the sky or the foliage of trees straight onto a space on the wall, like a picture. Caught in a stream of sunlight, mirror glass is immediately reminiscent of water – the surface of a pool or lake. Although mirrors have an obvious function in reflecting back our own images to allow personal adjustments, these other qualities are the reason they are often used for purely decorative effect and at heights above eye level.

Metal and wirework may be reflective if left unpainted; but even when covered over, these materials have an airy quality, with their bends and twists and filigrees that allow light to shine through the spaces in their structures. Cast iron, which has been used since the 16th century for firebacks and cooking utensils, became an enormously versatile medium once industrial manufacture was possible. It has a compressed strength that makes it an ideal building material, and it was used extensively for fences and balconies of terraces and villas in the 18th and 19th centuries. Its manufacture also meant that delicate patterns could be made repeatedly, resulting in a material that combined function with ornament better than any other. Ornament was suddenly cheaply available to everybody, and was seen decorating the exteriors of houses and street furniture with moulded patterns of acanthus leaves, grapevines and flowers.

Wrought iron, cut from sheet metal, is more malleable than cast iron, but less strong. It was used for more elaborate ironwork balconies, gates and fences and for smaller decorative pieces designed for interiors. Candelabra, sconces, mirror frames and the like could be moulded with three-dimensional sprays of flowers and foliage in a wholly naturalistic manner.

light fittings

Glass chandeliers exploit all the qualities of candlelight. The flickering flames shine into the core of crystal pieces, bringing them to life like drops of dew or pieces of ice in the sunlight. The first entirely glass chandeliers made in

Europe were fashioned on the Venetian island of Murano in about 1700. They were developed into confections of coloured glass, some translucent, some opaque. Beautifully moulded flowers, such as carnations and pinks, and sinuous stems and leaves formed the arms of the candleholders. French designs were characterized by metalwork frames and rock crystal drops, and English pieces were made of moulded or reticulated glass from the 1720s.

By the late 18th century, huge hanging pieces with chains and festoons, drops and pendants were produced in quantity in styles that typify what we usually call to mind when we think of a chandelier. The extravagance of their glass and crystal ensured that the light provided before the advent of electricity by a few candles (which were themselves a significant domestic expense) was multiplied to the greatest possible extent. Some of the names given to the shapes of the chandelier drops make clear their naturalistic inspiration – for example, 'icicle' for long, thin, tapered, pointed and multi-faceted drops; and 'pear' for pieces shaped like the fruit.

Following the production of the first commercial electric light bulb in 1881, the electric light fitting became a new area of opportunity for designers. By the 1890s, there was an understandable obsession with design for electricity, which revolutionized the appearance of towns and cities. Electric light was available for street lamps, shops, theatres and lighthouses, as well as domestic rooms. A dark 19th-century world suddenly came alight. Some of the first domestic designs featured incandescent bulbs inside globular glass shades, while others combined with metal to make modern chandeliers. Manuals explaining a domestic electricity system proliferated.

BELOW Inspired by Japanese room screens, these lampshades are made from modelling wood and thin paper. Light shines softly through the paper and brightly through the holes cut to form patterns of foliage and daisy flowers. The result is a simple but effective, *quasi*-Oriental design.

Soon the shades on incandescent lamps took on the forms of flowers, the most obvious being that of a bellflower, rounded at the base and fluted at the wider, opening edge – the perfect shape to contain a bulb and distribute the light. Architects and designers who were part of the Arts and Crafts movement were working at exactly this point in history, and beautiful examples of early electric fittings can still be seen in their houses. The sunflower – a favourite motif of the Aesthetic movement, which influenced many Arts and Crafts designers – was used for wall-mounted uplighters. These cast shadows in the shape of sunflowers on the ceiling.

In the century since then, all manner of materials have been used to make shades for electric light, reaching, perhaps, a high point with glass and metal in the Art Deco period and a low point in the 1970s with crochet and macramé – materials that did not work well with light sources. Less than 150 years after the first light bulb, electric light is still an area that attracts a great deal of design talent, and there is an ever-growing number of ingenious contemporary solutions on the market. Many of these have been inspired by organic natural forms, and some have an air of mystery that is totally in keeping with the luminous qualities of light.

BELOW LEFT A plain and traditional lampshade is decorated in restrained English chintz style with hand-painted sweet peas.

BELOW RIGHT A modern standard lamp pretends to be a tree: the trunk is covered with willow twigs bound together with twine, and the shade is decorated with a border of real leaf skeletons.

detail

Much of the colour and pattern that surround us inside the home is found in the detail of interiors, in the practical and ornamental objects on display. Many of these objects reflect back imagery of the outside world, either by their shape or by their applied decoration. In fact, so all-pervasive is this inspiration that it would be a considerable task to try to accumulate only objects devoid of a hint of nature. A quick look around almost any room will discover images of flowers, foliage, fruits, stars, animals – something that connects us with a wider landscape.

silverware The shapes and surface decorations of silver have a long history of naturalism, exhibiting some of the prettiest flower and fruit motifs of all ornamental wares. European silverware in the 17th century was characterized by accurately drawn flowers in imitation of the detailed work of Dutch still-life paintings. Such decoration was either embossed (that is, modelled in relief by working with a hammer and punches on the back of sheet metal) or chased (chiselled) into the face of the metal. The late 17th-century fashion for all things Chinese influenced the floral and landscape designs on silver, giving way in the early 18th-century to elaborate rococo embossed floral decoration. By the mid-19th century, naturalism dictated form as well as decoration, resulting in a fashion for silverware moulded and embossed in the shapes of fruit such as apples and pears.

One of the most influential metalwork designers working at the end of the 19th century was Christopher Dresser, who made an intensive study of plants, developing an idea of 'artistic botany' that linked art to science. He analysed the structure of plants in microscopic detail, noting the geometry of the symmetrical sections, and creating a new philosophy and practice of art and craftsmanship which he hoped would be suitable for the industrial age. The result was a new style of ornamentation that evolved directly, as he claimed, from 'natural laws'. Dresser

RIGHT These Persian buttercups, with their finely chiselled shapes, illustrate the direct inspiration that an artist can draw from nature. It is easy to make the visual jump from petal to metal when looking at these flowers.

BELOW LEFT An English silver bowl dating from 1895 with a naturalistic embossed design of roses is polished to a fine lustre. Such decorative silver and silver-plated wares reflected the Victorian taste for opulence.

BELOW CENTRE A collection of beautiful spoons demonstrates the skill and versatility of the silversmith. The superb serving spoon in the centre, embossed with foliage and flowers, dates from about 1819, and the shell-shaped tea-caddy spoon on the right was made in about 1850.

worked in electroplated silver, producing pieces of stunning modernity that were functional, geometric and undecorated but also organic, based on a deep understanding of plant forms.

Silver is an ideal medium for sinuous organic designs, and in consequence some of the finest plant-inspired decorative pieces have been achieved in this medium. Art Nouveau silver, for example, often displays decorative art at its very best, in naturalistic and curvilinear forms decorated with Japanese-inspired motifs of flowers and birds. Many of the great European names in design can be found attributed to such silverwares, including those of C R Ashbee, Archibald Knox, René Lalique, Georg Jensen, Charles Rennie Mackintosh, Josef Hoffmann and Otto Wagner. Wonderfully elaborate silver was crafted in the American workshops of Louis Comfort Tiffany, and the London shop Liberty's commissioned and sold accomplished Art Nouveau and Arts and Crafts silver and pewter.

BELOW RIGHT A three-piece tea set made in the 1920s takes the form of pumpkins, with a chased surface pattern that provides decoration and also gives an impression of the texture of the vegetable skin.

enamelware Not all consumers could afford expensive gold or silver items, or even those made of less precious metals. In the 19th century, affluent households were able to replace their old iron cooking pots with lighter, more practical copper and brass utensils. But despite their industrial manufacture, these were expensive domestic commodities, and they have survived only as a result of time-consuming scouring and polishing by domestic staff. Enamelware was developed as a cheap alternative to copper and brass. A thin sheet of tin was cut out with shears into a shape around a template, then curved around and soldered together to create the finished pot, pan, jug, mug or plate. The shiny enamel surface was produced by bonding coloured glass in powder form to the metal by firing at high temperatures.

Enamelware was sometimes left as one plain colour or it was decorated with abstract or floral motifs, depending on the country and region from which it originated. The overpainted floral patterns have a naivety that is in keeping with the modest functionality of these pieces – a naturalistic flower spray or two, or a stylized border, and very little more. Most striking about enamelware, though, are its vibrant colours – sunny sky blues, gentle leaf and grass greens, or the intense bright blues and reds of garden flowers, which would have cheered up a sombre kitchen. The wares provided a way of bringing colour inside workaday rooms that would otherwise probably have had very little of ornamental interest.

LEFT This diverse collection of enamelware shows the variety of effects that have been used as decoration: some is plain, some has linear or checked geometric pattern and some is floral. The large jug is decorated with a stencilled design of roses, and in the top right-hand corner a coffee pot with a hand-painted floral decoration can be glimpsed.

BELOW A row of antique enamelled coffee pots and cafetières includes three floral patterns in differing styles: on the left, a highly stylized design of daisies and leaves; at centre right, an accomplished freehand pattern of honeysuckle; and on the far right, a later and less successful pattern of unidentifiable buds.

paraphernalia Once household implements are in place and domestic tasks are complete, the pleasure gained from making use of leisure time can lead to ornamentation for its own sake. Just as the ladies of affluent 16th-century households used their embroidery skills to enhance the look of their textiles, so homemakers over the centuries have enjoyed applying decoration to mundane objects and introducing elements that are purely ornamental. Decoration inspired by nature brings the landscape and the garden symbolically within the confines of the house, strengthening the link between indoors and out.

The choice of naturalistic decoration is very personal, revealing a great deal about the individual who makes the selection. One person might choose a piece of modern ceramic sculpture in an organic form, for example, while another might be interested in the exact renditions of botanical prints, and yet another might exhibit a sentimental attachment to the floral chintz designs of an idealized cottage garden. The traditionalist, the modernist, the scientist and the environmentalist will all have

BELOW LEFT A range of artists' sketchbooks and notebooks has been ingeniously covered with paper photocopies of floral textiles. The textures of the weaves are still visible and the floral patterns translate well to the new medium.

BELOW RIGHT Old shelves here carry a weight of nostalgia for the country cottage garden, with floral paper used to cover boxes and books, and chintz fabric employed for hanging storage bags. The rose theme is carried through to a real specimen and a postcard of a rose.

different interpretations of the natural world, which will affect how they decorate their interior landscapes and give a clue to their preoccupations.

For a great many people, the blooms of the flower garden are a decorative priority, as the books and folders covered with floral paper, the boxes carefully pasted with découpage and the bags sewn out of chintz on these pages show. Bright, cheerful and in full summer bloom, poppies, roses and daisies are the stalwart and pervasive motifs that have become synonymous with decorative tradition.

The attachment across continents, cultures and centuries to the image of the rose has resulted in thousands upon thousands of artistic interpretations of this one flower. It appears in bud, in full bloom, in exact detail and at every degree of stylization, right through to something angular and almost unrecognizable. It has been adopted to symbolize emotion, religion, politics and national identity, becoming much grander than a mere plant. Its image simply never leaves the stage – flower power indeed!

RIGHT A wooden box is treated to a crackle-glazed paint effect to simulate age and is découpaged with carefully cut-out and coloured poppies, iris, rose and tulips. The addition of butterflies and insects gives the piece the feel of a 17th-century Dutch still-life.

FAR RIGHT The real thing by the side of the poppy box gives an idea of the naturalistic detail that artists employ to draw and paint flower specimens.

Bringing the

Outside In

PREVIOUS PAGES
Blossom and flowering
bulbs placed in clear
glass containers in a
sunny window create
a light-filled display
redolent of spring.

LEFT Although there are
no flower arrangements
here, the products of
nature – fresh green
leaves in a vase; dried
twigs, ferns and
seedheads; fir cones;
ornamental gourds;
and a sculptural shell –
are brought inside in
profusion.

BELOW Far from being
a mere mass of dull and
dusty greenery, a pot
plant can be a thing of
contemporary beauty,
delicate and floral.

When we cut or buy flowers for the home or for gifts, we are concerned with the colours, shapes and scents of the blooms, but we pay little attention to any meaning that might be attached to individual species. There are exceptions, such as red roses that still speak of romance or white lilies that are sometimes still associated with mourning, but the language of flowers has been largely forgotten.

Our ancestors, though, would have been wholly aware of the symbolism of flowers, and of trees and fruits. Back in the 13th century, for example, the tulip, with its 'black heart behind shiny cheeks', was a symbol of hypocrisy. Round floral shapes, such as the rose or the daisy, represented the sun and were therefore associated with prosperity. Fruits with evident seeds, such as pomegranates, grapes, melons and figs, were symbols of fertility. To a medieval observer, nature was a background to personal emotions, and its beauties were significant.

By the 19th century, flowers had become overlaid with complicated sentimental and religious meanings. Interpretations differed, depending upon the beliefs of the commentator. S W Partridge, writing about the Christian language of flowers in 1857, has ivy representing an instructive charity: 'Thou lendest beauty to decay and death,/And throw'st a loveliness round loveless things./Yes, I will learn from thee.' His tulip is a symbol of pride – 'Thou art a flaunter' – and holly is cheerfulness in adversity as it 'braves the pelting storm'.

In efforts of interpretation, others scoured poetical works, especially those of Shakespeare, for the meaning of flowers. Note was taken, for instance, that it was the juice of the pansy, 'love-in-idleness', that made Titania fall for the first creature she saw, the absurd donkey-headed Bottom, on awakening in *A Midsummer Night's Dream*. And who could forget images of the doomed Ophelia in *Hamlet*, giving gifts of the sad flowers of her madness – rosemary for remembrance; pansies for thoughts; and rue, the herb of grace. Although it may be disappointing that these meanings have fallen into disuse, we can at least now choose blooms to grow and to bring indoors for their own qualities rather than for those we choose to cast upon them.

spring

There is a certain excitement in bringing fresh flowers into the house in spring after a long winter. They are a sign that clement weather is on the way, that we can begin to live outdoors again. The influential garden designer Gertrude Jekyll was concerned not just with gardens but also with cut-flower arrangements. In her 1907 book, *Flower Decoration in the House*, she is keen to promote the decorative use of spring flowers:

'I always think that this… is the season of all the year when the actual arranging of flowers affords the greatest pleasure. The rush and heat of summer have not yet come; the days are still fairly restful, and one is glad to greet and handle these early blossoms.'

Jekyll suggests arrangements of magnolia, arum lilies, daffodils, anemones, violets, hellebores and plum blossom in early spring, to be followed by wallflowers, tulips, jonquils, lily of the valley, lilac, Solomon's seal and laburnum later in the season.

In seeking to liberate garden design and flower arrangements from the formal approach that had dictated acceptable taste and fashion, Gertrude Jekyll had an enormous effect on our choice and handling of flowering plants. Victorian attitudes towards flower arranging were typified by a Miss Maling, writing in 1862. She concentrates at length on the creation of highly structured wreaths and bouquets before arriving at a virtual footnote about designs in 'Upright Flower Vases'. She is almost dismissive: 'Any common flowers do very well in this way. Very choice things,

RIGHT Gertrude Jekyll would have approved of the reflective hammered-silver bowl that is used for this powerful arrangement of highly scented jonquils and tuberoses backed by shiny berried ivy: she promoted the use of unfussy, undecorated containers.

FAR RIGHT An ancient terracotta pot of white daffodils is placed at the back of a table arrangement of hyacinths growing in a collection of different water-pots. The look is contemporary, but such a design would not have looked amiss on a Victorian window-sill.

indeed, are rather wasted for such a purpose; while a close mass of common flowers will, at a little distance, answer extremely well.' Jekyll had no such qualms – in fact, she relished free and unstructured interpretations of common garden and wild flowers overflowing from simple 'upright' vases. We owe her a great debt for encouraging the simplicity and informality that characterize flower arrangements today.

Flowering bulbs are the plants we associate most strongly with spring. Their blooms tend to have strong shapes, colours and perfume, which would suggest simple monochrome or scented designs. Minimalist interiors can take advantage of flowering bulbs in every shade of white – snowdrops, narcissi, tulips, hyacinths, crocus, cyclamen – offset by green stems and foliage. These white-only decorations avoid introducing colour to a carefully balanced and muted room.

In interiors that call for drama, tulips are ideal. One of the world's major commercial flower crops, the hundred or so species run into literally thousands of cultivars, with new ones developed each year. There is a colour to suit every taste and decorating scheme, from brilliant reds, yellows and oranges to contrast or coordinate with a room, to soft apricots, mauves and creamy pinks for a more gently harmonious effect. Tulips can stand alone in a clear glass vase, or be mixed in great bunches with waxy dark green foliage or geometric spears of pussy willow or blossom twigs.

Although the Victorians approached flower arranging with considerable strictness and restraint, they were, paradoxically, very keen on unruly potted plants, grown on window-sills or in the newfangled glass and cast-iron conservatories that graced the backs of affluent villas. Among the more exotic palms, citrus trees and camellias that could now be grown in pots, Victorian commentators advocated the cultivation inside of 'Dutch bulbs' – tulip, hyacinth, crocus, jonquil, narcissus. Today there is something of a revival in the fashion for displaying growing plants, either in specially designed water-pots or in attractive containers. Just as our 19th-century forebears were excited by new technology that allowed affordable glasshouse extensions, we in turn are preoccupied with 'garden rooms' that will link the house to the garden.

ABOVE A small green-glass tumbler of spring flowers, including narcissi and grape hyacinths, acquires instant glamour with a hanging bell of snake's head fritillary, one of the rarest wild flowers. The one pictured here is a cultivated bloom, with another fritillary, the mysteriously nicknamed 'fox's grapes', behind.

LEFT A deceptively simple decoration with white spring flowers is actually an extravagant selection of orchids and cut jonquils, amaryllis and agapanthus.

summer

Summer has flowering plants of every colour and tone, an abundance that encourages a more opulent and mixed approach to flower design than in spring. However, in the 19th century a love of colour and copious decoration was, as we have seen, a source of angst to purists. Our Miss Maling of 1862 has many a cautionary word to say about colour in ornamental flowers. For example, she advises: 'Much may be done... by avoiding contrasts – or rather, I should say, comparisons of tint – by bringing in those touches which really soften, and seeking for soft and harmonious blending of the shades, rather than as now, for strong and startling effects of colour.' On this, at least, Gertrude Jekyll broadly agrees: 'The garden artist... will be able to put together a wider range of colour material, and yet keep within safe limits. But it needs the keen and well-trained colour eye.'

This is, of course, just the sort of decorating advice that strikes fear in the heart of the amateur designer. What is a 'keen and well-trained colour eye' and do I have one? Or, rather, do I have a dull or even vulgar colour eye? In short, we are afraid even today that our bad taste might let us down in the eyes of those that spy our interiors or our flower arrangements.

However, there are several encouraging considerations here. Firstly, bad taste is now often good taste – that is, kitsch arrangements of strong colours, such as orange and purple accented with yellow, are fashionable. After all, the ability to recognize kitsch and then confidently flaunt it puts you one step ahead in the taste game. Secondly, seasonal flowers, particularly home-grown rather than shop-bought combinations, go together effortlessly in nature, so you are, in fact, unlikely to go too far wrong. You only have to imagine a summer flowering meadow, complete with every colour of the rainbow, to relax about complex combinations of shades – and, perhaps, to note that a predominance of restful green background grass is a great colour mediator.

LEFT Backed by a brilliant pink hydrangea bush, this outdoor table is decorated with a jug of bright mauve mallow flowers and overflowing bowls of shiny, colourful cherries.

BELOW Old-fashioned summer garden flowers – roses, scabious and blue agapanthus – are given a modern look arranged in separate clear glass vases and then grouped together.

Essentially, though, a 'colour eye' – for flower arrangements or for any aspect of interior design and decoration – can be developed only by a great deal of looking. Taking note of colour combinations in gardens, whether domestic or grand, in flower designs done by professionals or by friends, or in designs pictured in books and magazines, will give a feel of what works and what doesn't – and of what you like and what you don't. Essentially, it is important to shake off preconceived ideas and allow yourself freedom of design. Gertrude Jekyll was celebrating such liberation back in 1907, so we can surely take it properly on board nearly a century later:

'...we are no longer under the tyranny of any generally-prevailing fashion as to what we are to put as flower-decoration in our rooms. We have shaken off our fetters; we can determine for ourselves and decide what is beautiful and desirable, and think with only repulsion of being bound by any prevailing fashion.'

The soft-edged petals and forms of summer blooms, many also characterized by groupings of flower heads on a single stem, are often at their best when massed together. If colour combinations are still a worry, look for similar tone – that is, intensity of shade. Bright, clear colours go together well, as do softer mid-tones: for example, the strong blues of delphiniums look good with clear bright pink roses; while the dusky mauves of scabious are ideal with the paler pinks of peonies.

The message of freedom of design and an anything-goes approach to the natural world brought inside is amply illustrated on these pages. Brilliant summer flowers are arranged with apparent abandon alongside fruits of the season, and at the other extreme – and the other end of the colour spectrum – beachcombers' finds are simply brought inside as decoration. Fossils and shells and sea-washed wood are organic, relying on a natural geometry of shape that is a completely different sort of ornamentation to that of copious summer flowers. The unadorned patterns of nature, particularly the spirals of shells and ammonites, speak for themselves.

BELOW LEFT Driftwood is beautiful for its soft, washed-out colours and its water-sculpted, rounded shapes. It also has associations of expansive adventure, as its formation requires long travels across the sea.

BELOW Discovering an ammonite in a rock face is an enormous thrill, but they are hard to find and expensive to buy. These are plaster casts of ammonites, laid as a feature pavement in a patio garden room.

RIGHT Shells are the bargains of the ornamental world: they are beautiful decorative objects found for free, reminders of summer holiday relaxation. If you need to create the illusion, they are inexpensive to buy.

autumn

LEFT This design, apart from the centrally placed newsprint 'laurel wreath', looks casual, but in fact its organic elements have been very carefully chosen for their shapes and colours, which work brilliantly against the pale green wall.

BELOW Pumpkins used to be found for sale in greengrocers, but they are now just as likely to be seen in fashionable florists' windows. Their wonderful shapes and deep matt colours have great decorative potential.

Flower arrangements made from garden or wild flowers – rather than shop varieties that disregard the actual season – can look melancholy, even tatty by the time autumn arrives. Late roses have lost the vigour and sunshine of the summer, and the late flowerings of the herbaceous border begin to show their age: a few blooms left among the seedheads.

To make matters worse, we now have a strange relationship with the stalwarts of early autumn, dahlias and chrysanthemums. The dahlia, a native of Mexico adored by the Victorians for its exoticism and striking colour, went spectacularly out of fashion, having been criticized for its over-bright, scentless and stiff petals and its rigid-looking stem and leaves. It has recently seen something of a revival, though, particularly with the hugely successful introduction of a cultivar called 'Bishop of Llandaff', which has managed to develop a trendy character in its small, slightly irregular, dark scarlet blooms. As a result, the dahlia is now seen blooming happily again in mixed garden borders and arranged, sometimes as a mass of close-knit, one-colour pom-poms, in contemporary displays.

The rise and fall of the fashion for chrysanthemums is rather more mysterious. The plant has been cultivated in China since 500 BC and by the 13th century there were as many as 70 varieties. It had a medicinal use – dew gathered from chrysanthemum flowers was said to preserve and restore vitality. It also exerted a constant fascination for artists, becoming a favourite decorative motif in China, where it symbolized autumn, joviality and an easy life. Along with the peony, its proliferation in the Chinese decorative arts, particularly ceramics, sparked a similar fashion across Europe for the flower as a decorative motif during the vogue for chinoiserie. The garden flower itself was brought by a plant hunter to Europe in 1860 and became enormously popular, spawning gardening societies devoted exclusively to the species.

All was well at that point, particularly as the Victorian language of flowers credited the chrysanthemum with the symbolism of optimism, truth and even love. The problems with its use in flower arrangements began when it became associated with funerals, perhaps because its sombre colours and earthy smell were thought appropriate to the occasion. Bringing chrysanthemums indoors was deemed unlucky, a symbol of death. Some of this dismal image still lingers today, perhaps not quite recognized but just felt by subconscious association.

Yet the chrysanthemum remains irresistible. Its deep scarlet, russet orange and faded peach blooms are reminiscent of the colours of autumn leaves; and its distinctive scent is permeated with childhood memories of the smell of bonfires as the garden is prepared for winter. The very name of the flower is tied up with our culture, being the subject at one time or another of every school English spelling test. And the chrysanthemum petals, valued and explored for centuries by artists of both East and West, still uncurl beautifully in a vase.

The autumn arrangements shown here offer plenty of ornamental alternatives to flowers we might not feel comfortable with. The strongest of all autumnal associations is that of falling fruits and leaves, and there is no reason why these can't find their way directly into an interior. The harvest season is well represented by the gathering and simple display of the fallen elements of the natural world, or of the dried seedpods that come after colourful summer flowers. Bright colour can still be had from evergreen plants, and then there are all the shiny browns of cones and conkers and bare, leafless twigs. It takes some lateral thinking about what a 'flower arrange-ment' can be. The idea is transliterated into a bowl of orange and yellow gourds or a mantel of artlessly, but carefully, placed garden or woodland detritus. It is necessary, perhaps, to have firmly in mind Gertrude Jekyll's words about shaking off the fetters, deciding for ourselves what is beautiful and justly decorative – and then to go for it.

RIGHT Three ways to make the very best of what is left in the autumn garden are demonstrated here in heads of dried hydrangeas, a wreath of dried berries and a contemporary picture made from a few leaves mounted on handmade paper.

winter

Having struggled with designs for the shortening days of autumn, most of the 19th-century flower-arranging manuals seem to give up altogether when they reach winter. Apart, presumably, from the assumption that the usual pagan accoutrements of holly, ivy and mistletoe will be hijacked for the Christmas and New Year period, there are blank months.

The 20th-century writers become a bit braver. Constance Spry, writing in 1937, comments on winter decoration with some spirit:

'It is not easy perhaps at this season to make good effects and one must plan one's indoor decorations with care, but for all that there is no need to sink, under a glut of greenhouse chrysanthemums, to the level of dullness and indifference. I rather enjoy the first decorations of winter. The limitation imposed by the scarcity of flowers causes one to have a watchful eye for everything of delicate outline or vigorous shape which will add to our flower arrangements.'

LEFT Dramatic 'architectural' arrangements of twigs with coloured bark and pussy willow are complemented by silver-birch logs propped against the wall. There is no intention of using these as fuel – one has even become an ingenious photo-holder.

RIGHT A 21st-century Christmas room incorporates lavish numbers of red and white anemones, traditional in colour but in fact out-of-season. These forced blooms would have been impossible to achieve in earlier centuries.

Spry advises against the random juxtaposition of a variety of seedheads and Chinese lanterns, which are devoid of necessary form when combined, to concentrate instead on more unusual dried plants, including branches of larch cones and alliums.

Spry's visionary ideas about flower arranging seemed revolutionary at the time, but are no longer so. The clues that she offers here were, gradually, taken on board by later 20th-century floral designers, so that today we are totally at home with the once unusual sight of a spray of bare twigs on their own in a vase.

This idea sometimes now reaches mammoth proportions, with huge branches and logs incorporated as part of the decoration, particularly in high-ceiling or double-height rooms where they can be used to full dramatic effect. It is no coincidence that large portions of forest should now be found in such stark interior spaces. At one time we sought sanctuary from the Wild Wood within the confines of an enclosed garden, but once thoroughly enclosed in a gardenless apartment, we crave a sense of wildness and open air. So we drive out of town, plunder the wild, and haul it back inside. This is, paradoxically, an essentially urban style: only in town would a log be purely decorative – in the country it would find its way onto the fire instead.

To the extent that conscience allows, we have a no-holds-barred attitude to culling anything with ornamental potential from nature. Flower shops are now full of all manner of curious material, some imported and unfamiliar, some local but suddenly exposing its decorative potential. Bits of bark, extraordinary dried mosses, huge and exotic empty seed-cases, dried fungi, nuts – all are now almost as much a part of the floral repertoire as blooms themselves. Even the words 'flower arranging' now seem antiquated and inappropriate, begging to be replaced with something more properly descriptive, such as 'organic design' or 'plant interpretation'. Certainly, we have come a long way in shedding those fetters that restricted earlier approaches to the ornamental use of the treasures of the outdoors inside our homes.

LEFT Back to the future here, with a mouth-watering profusion of pyracantha berries and rosehips that achieves a gothic and modern atmosphere at one and the same time. The rich effect is highlighted with touches of gold and with candlelight.

index

Photographic Acknowledgments

Caroline Arber 1, 14 (bottom), 19, 23 (right), 24, 25, 27, 50, 51 (right), 68, 70 (right), 83, 86, 114, 115 (left), 115 (right), 124, 138, 149 (top), 150
Jan Baldwin 79, 94, 95 (right), 131 (left)
Tim Beddow 21, 61, 62, 120 (right)
Mark Bolton 15, 99 (Garden Picture Library)
Nick Brown 35 (right)
Simon Brown 109 (right)
Linda Burgess 146
Charles Colmer 17, 34, 40, 76, 98, 123, 126, 147, 148 (left), 155
Harry Cory-Wright 47, 55 (right), 91 (left), 91 (right), 95 (left), 134, 135
Christopher Drake 2-3, 14 (top), 29, 37, 41, 48, 49 (right), 74 (left), 74 (right), 75, 100, 102, 111 (left), 111 (right), 137 (left)
Melanie Eclare 127 (right)
Andreas von Einsiedel 46, 66 (bottom right)
Polly Eltes 64, 131 (right), 153
Craig Fordham 39
Kate Gadsby 112 (left), 113 (right)
David George 56 (right), 59, 129, 142
Catherine Gratwicke 119, 145
Huntley Hedworth 12, 143
Jacqui Hurst 44, 84 (top), 107 (right)
Sian Irvine 113 (left)
Hugh Johnson 101
Andrea Jones 149 (bottom)
Sandra Lane 87 (left), 87 (right)
Mark Luscombe Whyte 140

Simon McBride 110
Jill Mead 28 (top), 55 (inset)
James Merrell 6, 7, 18, 32, 38, 49 (left), 51 (left), 53 (right), 54, 54 (inset), 57, 65 (right), 71, 77, 85 (left), 103, 106, 108, 109 (left), 116, 118, 120 (left), 121, 125, 136 (left), 136 (right), 137 (right), 141, 154
Tham Nhu Tran 10, 43
Michael Paul 60 (right), 128
Bridget Peirson 31, 56 (left)
Clay Perry 4-5, 23 (left), 78, 127 (left)
Stephen Robson 89
Heini Schneebeli 16 (right), 36, 151
William Shaw 66 (top right)
Ron Sutherland 30
Debi Treloar 16 (left), 28 (bottom), 33, 35 (inset), 42, 53 (left), 96, 130, 144
Pia Tryde 8, 9, 20, 29, 26 (left), 26 (right), 58, 66 (left), 70 (left), 72, 73, 80 (left), 80 (centre), 80 (right), 81, 82 (bottom), 85 (right), 88, 90, 92, 112 (right), 132, 133 (top), 133 (bottom left), 133 (right), 156
Simon Upton 52
Ling Wong 65 (left), 107 (left), 107 (centre)
Polly Wreford 108 (centre)

Stylists: Carl Braganza, Ben Kendrick, Hester Page, Kristin Perers, Pippa Rimmer, Gabi Tubbs

Designer-makers: Belinda Ballantyne, Jane Cassini, Nicola Holbrooke, Jayne Keeley, Sandra Lee

Further Reading

Dresser, Christopher, *Principles of Decorative Design*, London, 1873
Eastlake, Charles L., *Hints on Household Taste*, London, 1868
Evans, Joan, *Nature in Design*, Oxford, 1933
Garfield, Simon, *Mauve*, London, 2000
Ionides, Basil, *Colour and Interior Decoration*, London, 1926
Jekyll, Gertrude, *Flower Decoration in the House*, London, 1907
Jones, Owen, *The Grammar of Ornament*, London, 1856
Pavord, Anna, *The Tulip*, London, 1999
Rees, Ronald, *Interior Landscapes*, Baltimore, 1993
Thomas, Keith, *Man and the Natural World*, London, 1983